"Networking is really the process of contacts that, if nurtured, will grow a relationship added to the web attracts new referrals and networking relationship. Most of my best clients were referred to me by someone two or three referrals removed from the initial contact or relationship. It is a career long process with substantial rewards for those dedicated to the effort and the excellent service that must accompany it."

        Ron Mills CPA, CFP - Partner
        Carr, Riggs & Ingram, LLC
        Nashville, TN

"Effective networking is a process that is at once both predictable and random: good networking habits will predictably build relationships required for business success – but it is the random nature of unforeseen connections – and subsequent opportunities that for me, provides the freshness, the motivation, and the enthusiasm for every meeting, every follow-up, and every communication."

        Joe Thompson - President
        Pinpoint Profiles, LLC
        Nashville, TN

"When you meet someone new, think of them as someone you may want to refer. Learn everything you can about their business by asking questions as if you were a potential client. This technique provides me with a list of "go to" suppliers for every area a client may need. Not only is my client more reliant on me to help meet their needs, but I have someone who is more likely to think of me when a need arises that I can assist with."

        Donna Griggs - President
        E-3 Performance Group
        Nashville, TN

"Networking is not something you do, it's something you are. Networking is the mindset of looking for connections between people and ideas. The right connections can come at any time, at any place. If you become a networker of people and ideas, you'll be amazed how it adds value to your life . . . intellectually, emotionally, and financially."

        Jim Cumbee JD, MBA - Managing Director
        Tennessee Valley Group, Inc.
        Nashville, TN

"Networking is a process and commitment. Learning how to connect and network, in the long run, is the most effective way to build one's business."

        Joseph F. Fragnoli, CPA - Senior Tax Manager
        Blankenship CPA Group, PLLC
        Brentwood, TN

"Smart people know that the real marketing opportunity lies in how to leverage networking to achieve their goals. It's your focus on the strategy and its successful execution that is important, not the focus on the end game."

Joel Widmer - CEO
Fluxe Digital Marketing
Nashville, TN

"Effective networking is the fastest way for a salesperson, manager, or business owner to improve their net worth! Effective networkers focus on giving rather than getting. A good mantra to follow is get what you want by giving others what they need."

John Boyens - CEO
BoyensGroup
Nolensville, TN

"If there's one thing I've learned in business, it's you can't advertise trust. The highest form of flattery is getting a referral. It's the lifeblood of my business, and a direct result of my networking efforts."

Dan Aronoff - Owner
FranNet of Middle and West Tennessee
Nashville, TN

"No matter how big or small your business is, your clients aren't doing business with your business – they're doing business with YOU. In other words, it's the power of the relationships you build through your connections that make the difference – and that's the power of networking."

Cindy Beresh-Bryant - President
HR Solutions by Design, LLC
Culleoka, TN

"Successful networking happens by building meaningful relationships in a purposeful and disciplined way. Today more than ever, we do business and build relationships with those whom we trust. We also expect time spent with others to add value to our lives. So, be clear about what makes you trustworthy and what defines the value you bring to each person you meet. Then set yourself apart by following up and delivering on promises that you make to every person, every time."

Terry Humphrey - Principal
Terry Humphrey, LLC
Nashville, TN

THE MINDSET OF NETWORKING®
A formal and disciplined approach to networking

Unlocking the Secrets To Successful
Business-To-Business Networking

Stewart C. Ross

The Mindset of Networking® is a registered trademark of
Stewart C. Ross, Member, Southeast Business Forums, LLC.
Nashville, Tennessee
www.southeastbusinessforums.com

Copyright © 2013 by Stewart C. Ross

All rights reserved. No part of this book may be used or reproduced in any manner whatsoever without written permission except in the case of brief quotations embodied in critical articles and reviews.

Yooper Publications™ books may be purchased for educational, business, or sales promotional use. For information please write: Stewart C. Ross, Yooper Publications™, P.O. Box 158262, Nashville, TN 37215 or visit us at www.Southeastbusinessforums.com.

Front Cover designed by Fernando Boyd Greene.
Back Cover designed by Fernando Boyd Greene.
Editing by Dimples Kellogg.
Printed in the United States of America by Wax Family Printing, LLC. Murfreesboro, TN.

Library of Congress Cataloging-in-Publication Data

Ross, Stewart C.
The Mindset of Networking® / Stewart C. Ross.
Stewart C. Ross – 1st ed.
        p. cm.
    ISBN 978-0-9888851-0-3
     1. Non-Fiction 2. Business 3. Networking
DC

YOOPER PUBLICATIONS™, LLC
P.O. Box 158262
Nashville, TN 37215

www.YooperPublications.com

Distributed by Yooper Publications™, LLC

Southeast Business Forums, LLC
P.O. Box 158262
Nashville, TN 37215

Please visit us at
www.Southeastbusinessforums.com

Please visit our blog site:
www.themindsetofnetworking.com

To my friend

Robbins P. Bogue

Thank you, Robbie, for taking me under your wing all those years ago.
I'm sorry you didn't get to finish the race.

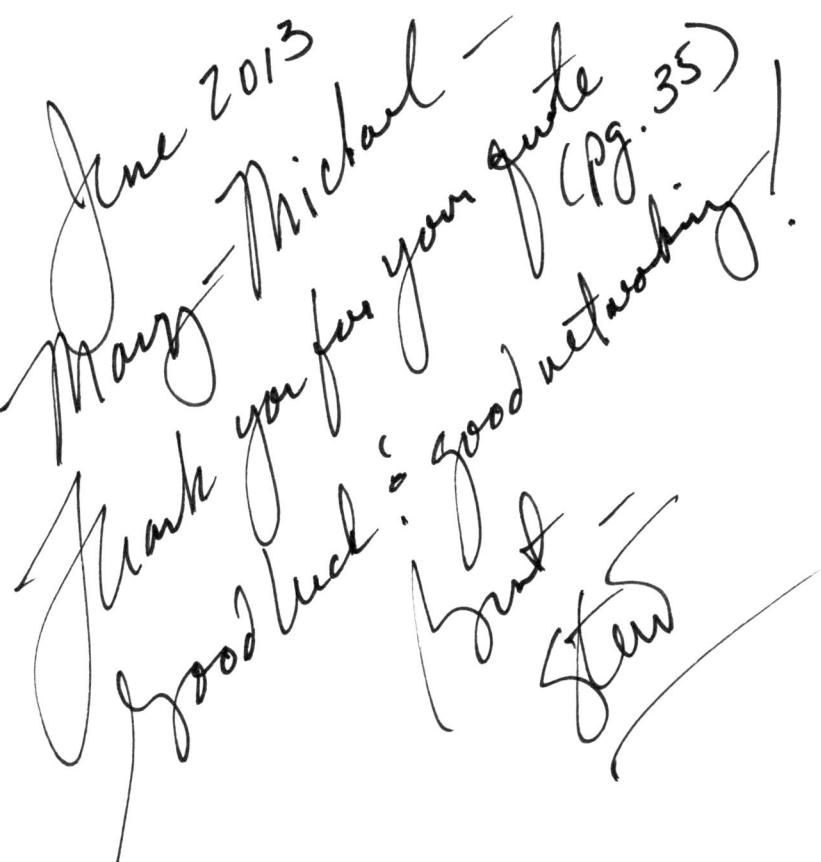

June 2013
Mary-Michael —
Thank you for your quote (pg. 35)
Good luck & good networking!
Best —
Steve

THE MINDSET OF NETWORKING®

A formal and disciplined approach to networking

- Contents -

Foreword 11

Introduction 15

One: The Mindset of Networking® 19

Two: What Are Your Networking Expectations? 27

Three: Which Networking Organizations Should I Join? 35

Four: Networking Protocol 51

Five: Reaching the Nirvana of Networking 61

Six: Social Capital and Social Competence 67

Seven: Networking Strategies 77

Eight: Networking Tactics 85

Nine: Troika Best Practices 99

Ten: One Last Piece of Advice 109

Appendix 113
    1. If I Can Do It, So Can You 113
    2. How to Construct an Effective Elevator Speech 115
    3. E-mail Introduction 121
    4. Response to an E-mail Introduction 122
    5. The "One-Sheet" and How to Construct It 122

- Foreword -

I spent thirty-one years as a commercial banker starting in 1979 with Bank of America and ending my career with a regional bank in 2010. In between, I held positions at various banks in operations, internal auditing, and for the last twenty-six years, middle-market commercial lending to corporate clients.

During that period, there were times that everyone faces . . . being knocked down and having to force yourself to get up, shake it off, and get on with whatever it is that you needed to do to survive. You know, the situations in life that help shape you and make you a better person on a personal basis as well as a professional basis.

One of those times came for me in 1991. I had to make the transition from being a portfolio banker (commonly known as a "skinner") to a relationship manager with marketing responsibilities (a "trapper"). Without a successful transition, I would likely have been out of a job.

I was lucky.

I was fortunate to have the type of personality that could successfully make the switch. Not many bankers that I ever knew can say or do that. It wasn't easy and it didn't happen overnight, but I also had the perseverance, especially in light of working for the Boss from Hell who did everything to block my efforts.

My realization that quality business could only come as a result of personal relationships drove me to seek and participate in high-level networking organizations. It was there that I learned how to effectively network. I was taught the protocol of networking. I learned that it was better to be a Giver than a Taker. I figured out that sitting behind a desk waiting for the phone to ring didn't develop personal relationships.

For the next twenty plus years, my success in banking was due to networking and establishing trust through the partnerships with my networking partners. In October 2006, Sandy and I moved to Nashville. She had worked for a large pet food company for thirty years, and the company decided to move the Los Angeles headquarters to Nashville, Tennessee. So I followed my wife (that's when I learned the phrase "trailing spouse") and left everything back in Southern California. I knew no one other than my wife. But when you essentially start over, you revert to the tactics and strategies that previously provided you with some measure of success. Unfortunately, there was no senior-level networking organization in Nashville. Networking in Nashville at that time was limited to the country club crowd (we call it the "Belle Meade" crowd here in Nashville), people you sit next to at church, and people you went to high school or college with (the Vanderbilt connection is very strong in Nashville as you can imagine).

My problem was that I had to book $10 million in loans each year. Sitting next to the local plumber, electrician, and hairdresser wasn't going to cut it. What they call "speed networking" was a waste of time. I never had very good business development experiences at the local chamber of commerce. I had to do something to create a vehicle for meaningful referrals.

Because of the influx of professionals to Nashville (similar to Sandy and me), I determined that Nashville was ready for a Business-to-Business senior-level networking organization. I was right.

So in January 2008, the first meeting of the Nashville Business Forum took place. By the second meeting, I had guests coming up to me telling me that our business model was what they had been looking for in Nashville but, up to this point, had not found. They all asked, "Where do I sign up?"

Today, Southeast Business Forums is seven chapters strong with approximately 160 members. Our culture promotes the establishment of deep and long-lasting relationships that over time will result in commerce. We also provide the resources of top professionals for our members to use to help them differentiate themselves from their competitors. Our philosophy is espoused by the tag line The Mindset of Networking®, which is the "formal and disciplined approach" to networking.

There are many people that I would like to thank but unfortunately there is not enough room in this book to do so. However, back in 1990, Robbie Bogue became a mentor to me through my involvement with Professional Network Group (PNG). He was instrumental in guiding me through the networking process and provided the encouragement to hang in there during the "mentoring" sessions with the Boss. Robbie died while training for a bicycle race in France.

I can't overlook thanking Davis Blaine and Gordon Gregory, the founders of Professional Network Group—now known as ProVisors. I cut my teeth on formal networking in PNG beginning in 1990. I was also a member of

Tracy Albert's group, The Newport Business Forum—now known as Business Forums International. Without those experiences I'm not too sure I would have survived in the New World of banking.

I'd also like to thank Carl DeVilbiss and Stan York. Both of these gentlemen have been part of the Southeast Business Forums. Carl and Stan linked together many of our networking presentations and determined that what we were really doing was presenting different components of a greater behavioral process called "social capital." I am especially grateful to Carl for his work on social capital and allowing me to use key parts of it in chapter 6.

There are too many members of Southeast Business Forums to thank and personally name here who assisted me in the transition of becoming an entrepreneur. However, my thanks go out to my members who provided direct quotations for the chapters of this book: Bill Watson, George Armistead, Jim Holmes, Margie Bingham, Carl DeVilbiss, Mary-Michael Horowitz, Steve Goldstein, Tim Stowell, Stan York, Steve Minucci, H A Beasley, and Leigh Ann Roberts. For their consultative roles, a thank you to Kevin Wax, Joel Widmer, Brent Baldwin, Neil Amrhein, John Lipinski, Laurie Hughes, John Boyens, and Fran Scott. Also a big thank you to Dimples Kellogg, my book coach and editor. I apologize in advance for not listing all of you. It's been a lot of fun, and without all of your support and wisdom, it wouldn't have been as fun or successful.

I would be remiss in not acknowledging my father, Patrick Ross, whose roots go back to where he was born and raised, the Upper Peninsula of Michigan. He is proud to be known as a Yooper.

There are not enough accolades to go around when it comes to my wife, Sandy. I was "retired" from banking in early 2010. Without Sandy, I could not have become a "kept man." Not only has my retirement allowed me to write this book but also pursue building Southeast Business Forums as well as write other books.

Stewart C. Ross
Nashville, TN
2013

- Introduction -

"You tend to do business with people that you like."

George Armistead
Armistead New Business Development
Nashville, TN

DEFINITION

NETWORKING, according to the *Merriam-Webster Dictionary*, is "the exchange of information or services among individuals, groups, or institutions; specifically: the cultivation of productive relationships for employment or business."

This is a book about a FORMAL NETWORKING PROCESS. If you follow the advice, guidelines, and protocol outlined in this book, you will increase your revenue. The process is not theoretical. It is a time-proven process that yields results. It has worked for me, and I've seen it work for others.

The process that you are about to learn comes directly from my experiences in selling as well as managing a formal networking organization and watching my members increase their revenue by practicing these tried-and-true networking fundamentals.

For most types of business, networking is the *most effective* way to develop your business and increase revenue.

HOWEVER . . .

For many people, networking is a very difficult thing to do effectively. Not all of us have networking in our DNA, nor do we feel comfortable learning how to do it and do it properly.

Are you **AN INTROVERT?** Well, either you'll have to get over it, teach yourself to get comfortable with networking, or hire someone who isn't an introvert and enjoys networking.

Are you **AN EXTROVERT?** If so, you are ahead of most of your competition.

Networking is like providing customer service. Good customer service can't be taught. It comes from within. The same goes for networking. I find that the good networkers and connectors seem to have the best customer service skills.

Yes, I can teach you how to answer the phone in a professional manner, but that's not real customer service. Yes, I can teach you the do's and don'ts of good networking, but I can't teach you to become comfortable with networking unless you are receptive and willing to learn. You will need to embrace networking. By embracing it, practicing it, and seeing the results, you will learn to become comfortable with networking.

STORY

I had to make the transition to sales or else I would lose my job. After years of being an "inside" banker, I had to quickly figure out how to transition to becoming a salesperson. So I joined several high-level networking organizations. After starting from scratch, within eighteen months, I landed the account of the largest machine shop in Southern California.

ADVICE

Here's what I learned. Although I was successful in teaching myself how to network and become comfortable in making it part of my daily routine, I recognized that many people cannot do that.

Introduction: The Mindset of Networking®

ADVICE

Very quickly, my historical comfort zone evaporated. I now did not want anything to do with the paperwork aspect of my job. Why? Because it interfered with my ability to be out calling on prospects, clients, and referral sources (now commonly known in the business world as Centers of Influence or COI). Once you get to that point, two things will have happened: you'll need to hire someone to do the paperwork for you, and you'll know that you've successfully transitioned to having networking as part of your DNA and making it part of your daily routine. In other words, it has become **FUN**.

CAUTION

Don't rely on networking as the only arrow in your marketing quiver!

With all of that being said, everyone networks, *INCLUDING YOU*. You may not think of it as networking, but most of your daily routine is exactly that. Whether it's standing in line at the grocery store and making small talk with others or participating in groups or organizations dedicated to networking, you're networking.

THE KEY TO YOUR BUSINESS NETWORKING SUCCESS will depend on your willingness to embrace networking and its protocol and make it part of your daily routine. It will depend on your ability to manage your time more effectively.

Networking is simply one word: *Communication.*

Simple idea, right?

Yes, it's plain common sense. I never could understand why so many smart people couldn't figure it out, especially my fellow bankers (but I used that to my advantage to differentiate myself from other bankers).

But the *Plan*, the *Strategy*, and the *Execution* of the communication will determine whether you will be successful. Networking, like many other things in life, is a **PROCESS**.

Communication in today's world is so much more complicated than in years past. Social media has created different ways to communicate. What happens when your team member who sits at the desk next to you needs to ask you a question but instead of turning to you and asking, he e-mails the question? Yes, that's a true story.

Of the comments, beliefs, or philosophies that I expound in this book, I will repeat one belief again and again because it is so important. That is, networking WAS, STILL IS, AND ALWAYS WILL BE on a *person-to-person* level, and for me that will be a face-to-face relationship.

I believe that unless you've got some networking blood in your system, it will be a tough hill to climb. If that's the case, then hire someone who does.

You've made the decision to invest time and money into improving your networking skills. Even if you take away only one thing from this book, you will increase your chances to improve your sales production.

Whether you are a W-2 employee or a business owner, increased networking behavior will lead to greater revenue, higher commissions, and/or larger bonuses than you've historically experienced. **I GUARANTEE IT.**

In this book I want to share with you the networking skills that I have learned over the years and help you learn how to use those skills to generate more business. The information here is bolstered by my experience in belonging to senior-level networking organizations and now running a senior-level professional service provider networking organization.

NOW I GET TO SHARE WITH YOU THE NETWORKING SECRETS THAT WILL MAKE YOU MORE SUCCESSFUL IN YOUR BUSINESS.

OH, ONE LAST QUESTION: How do you measure your networking success?

Answer: You Build More Relationships and Generate More Revenue.

- One -

The Mindset of Networking®

"Any business function is a process that can be modeled and continuously improved. The vast majority of my clients fail to recognize the importance of modeling SOCIAL processes, as well as operational and financial ones."

Carl DeVilbiss
Cooproductive
Nashville, TN

MAY I TAKE YOU ON A JOURNEY?

It is a journey that I've been on for more than twenty-two years, and I would like to share my ups and downs with you. It's been a lot of fun for me, and I know that it will be fun for you.

PLEASE JOIN ME ON THIS JOURNEY AS YOU LEARN HOW A FORMAL AND DISCIPLINED APPROACH TO NETWORKING WILL MAKE YOU MORE MONEY.

This is where it starts *WITH YOU!* It begins with your commitment to yourself to change your mindset regarding *NETWORKING*.

THE ENDGAME IS *INCREASED REVENUE*. It's about increased dollars in your employer's bank account, increased dollars in your pocket, and if you own your business, INCREASED REVENUE IN YOUR BANK ACCOUNT.

If you want to differentiate yourself from others who say they network, you will want to follow our program and our advice. You are about to be given a

ROAD MAP on how to increase your revenue by HAVING FUN.

Believe me, all people today say they *NETWORK*. And they are correct. It's true.

YOU NETWORK all day long. Whether you're standing in line waiting for a table at your favorite restaurant, sitting next to someone at your church or synagogue, texting family or friends, doing social media, or talking to your significant other or anyone else, YOU ARE NETWORKING.

I'm going to get it off my chest right up front. I believe that BUSINESS NETWORKING is done face-to-face, people actively engaged in listening. Social networking through technology is fine, but I'm convinced that in the business environment, it is less effective than the old, proven method of being in front of someone.

YET WHAT SEPARATES THE *BUSINESS* NETWORKERS FROM THE *SOCIAL* NETWORKERS?

A FORMAL AND DISCIPLINED APPROACH TO NETWORKING

Yes, to become an effective and productive business networker, you *MUST THINK* about what you are doing.

1. **KEEP SCORE**, even though there is not a formal scoreboard. In other words, keep in mind who you have referred business to. If you have given a number of referrals to someone without his reciprocating, you have two choices: give future referrals to someone else, or ask the person why he hasn't given you a referral. You WILL miss opportunities by not keeping score and expecting reciprocal behavior.
2. Follow **NETWORKING ETIQUETTE** and **PROTOCOL**. Your reputation will depend on it.
3. Approach **CONFLICT** and **CONFRONTATION** in a proper manner. Doing so can result in increased business and revenue.
4. **ACKNOWLEDGE** others, and provide TESTIMONIALS for them.
5. Use effective networking to **DIFFERENTIATE** yourself from the competition.
6. **EVALUATE** your networking activities continuously to ensure they are producing the desired results.
7. Build **TRUST** with others. Let others vouch for your credibility.
8. Build **PARTNERSHIPS** with others.

DEFINITION A *leads-oriented* networking organization is different from a *referral-oriented* organization. Typically, a leads-oriented networking organization will require its members to generate a minimum number of leads on a weekly or monthly basis. I believe that forcing people into a quota system will generate less than desirable leads. A referral-oriented networking organization will, over time, produce (without a quota system) meaningful referrals.

I'm telling you—NO, I'M GUARANTEEING YOU—that if you embrace our process, if you practice this process, and if you make formal networking a part of your daily routine, YOU WILL BECOME A TOP PRODUCER IN YOUR INDUSTRY AND MAKE MORE MONEY.

TEN YEARS AGO IT WAS **IMPORTANT** TO **DIFFERENTIATE** YOURSELF FROM THE COMPETITION.

TODAY, IT IS **CRITICAL** TO YOUR SURVIVAL TO **DIFFERENTIATE** YOURSELF.

The Great Recession resulted in many career W-2 corporate folks having the opportunity (usually not by their choice) to go out on their own as consultants. In past recessions, a thinning out process of competitors occurred. However, this recession has been different in that it has created an even greater number of competitors.

WHAT SEPARATES YOU FROM THE COMPETITION?

STORY Competition among banks is fierce. They are really only cannibalizing one another. So how does the smart banker keep clients from listening to other bankers who call on them?

The last thing you want is to be seen as a commodity service. In other words, as a banker, I never wanted to be seen merely as a conduit to money. At that point, I'm just a commodity, and there is NO DIFFERENTIATION from any other banker in the eyes of my clients.

So I taught myself to ask my clients if they had problems in other areas of their business (unrelated to banking). When I uncovered a problem, I told my client I could help him fix that problem by introducing him to a fellow networking professional. That person would come in and fix my client's problem professionally and expeditiously, and THOSE PROFESSIONALS MADE ME LOOK GOOD. All of a sudden, I was value added to my client and part of his team. No longer was I viewed as a commodity item. I did something the other bankers couldn't do. **I HAD DIFFERENTIATED MYSELF.**

ADVICE Use your networking organizations to help differentiate you from your competitors. Teach yourself to ask your clients where their problems are outside your area of expertise with the intent of introducing them to one of your networking partners.

WHAT ARE SOME TRAITS OF THE BEST NETWORKERS?

They Are Better Listeners.

"Listening is a competitive advantage."

H A Beasley
H A Beasley & Company, P.C.
Murfreesboro, TN

Are you are a good listener? Now be honest with yourself. Most of us aren't very good listeners. To become a good listener, you must (a) recognize that you aren't one, (b) teach yourself what it takes to be a good listener, and (c) practice being a good listener.

Do you tend to interrupt the conversation? Do you find yourself thinking ahead of the conversation and therefore not following what your conversation partner is saying? These are common traits of bad listeners.

 STORY One of my jobs in running the Southeast Business Forums is to interview potential guests to ensure that we find the right fit for the individual and for the organization. I was interviewing a young banker (a vice president no less) for the first time, and on three separate occasions during our discussion I reiterated that her next step would be to attend a chapter meeting as my guest. At the end of our meeting, she asked me what her next step should be.

 ADVICE The best salespeople will tell you that their secret lies in THEIR ABILITY TO LISTEN. Teach yourself to *LISTEN*. Don't interrupt the person you're talking with. Concentrate on what the person is saying rather than mentally jumping ahead of the conversation. Let the other person do most of the talking; remember, most people like to talk about themselves. Always maintain eye contact with the person you are talking with.

They Recognize The Power Of Good Networking Organizations.

Effective networkers know the power that a good networking organization can bring to them and their business. They know how to harness this power to build relationships and ultimately generate additional revenue.

STORY

I am fond of telling people that they have reached the *NIRVANA OF NETWORKING* when they can sit in front of clients or prospects and ask probing questions outside their areas of expertise for the purpose of identifying opportunities to introduce their friends into potential revenue situations.

ADVICE

Teach yourself to listen to people for the purpose of finding out how to properly identify an opportunity to introduce them into a potential revenue-generating situation. Don't be afraid to ask them what a good question would be to ask that would assist you in identifying that opportunity.

Teach yourself to ask your clients about their problems or issues outside your area of expertise. If you have followed the advice given above, you will be able to recognize opportunities to introduce your trusted friends into a potential revenue situation for them. At that point, you've done two things: (1) you become a trusted advisor to your client, and (2) your friend now owes you.

STORY

In Los Angeles (and I suspect other major urban areas like Chicago and New York), a business call is very surgical. In other words, the call does not last more than sixty minutes. The first five minutes are spent establishing credibility. The rest of the time is talking about business, why you are there, and whether you will be able to fix the prospect's problem. Not so in Nashville. The bulk of the time is spent in establishing your credibility that leads to you being viewed as a trusted person by the prospective client. THE RELATIONSHIP MATTERS.

ADVICE

Probably the greatest power of a networking organization is the ability of others to build your credibility with the person to whom they are introducing you. The person making the introduction has the ability to put you on a pedestal. He or she can eliminate the time you must take to establish your credibility with the prospective client. Make sure that this happens. Don't assume the person making the introduction does this as a matter of routine. Not everyone's networking skills are advanced to that point.

They Know That It Takes Time.

Networking has become a commodity service. If you want speed networking, leads-generating organizations, social networking disguised as business networking, quota systems, or other networking models that are not based on developing long-lasting and deep relationships, you run the risk of being a part of what I call a "*PREDATORY*" networking group. These are also organizations whose business models are basically geared toward "*TRANSACTIONAL NETWORKING.*"

STORY

I have a member who was considering joining one of the well-known women's networking organizations in Middle Tennessee. She went to her first meeting and met another professional service provider in the financial industry. This woman followed my member out to her car, trying to get her business.

It even got to the point that this woman was stalking my member at her other activities. Although this is an extreme example, it illustrates someone who, among other things, is not willing to take the time to establish a normal business relationship built on trust.

Be prepared to invest the time and energy necessary to build a trusting, respectful, and long-lasting business relationship. *ALWAYS, ALWAYS* go into networking with the attitude of being *A GIVER AND NOT A TAKER*.

They Know The Rules Of Effective Networking.

Effective networkers know the etiquette and protocol of networking. It's really only common sense. But for anyone who is common sense challenged the alternative is to teach yourself. I hope that you can connect with others in a good networking organization and learn from them. When you are deciding on which networking organization to join, find out what types of programs it has (if any) in place to assist you in learning the do's and don'ts of good networking.

TRUST ME, YOUR REPUTATION AND ULTIMATELY YOUR ABILITY TO GENERATE ADDITIONAL REVENUE WILL DEPEND ON THIS.

STORY

A member of the Southeast Business Forums made an introduction to a former member (he was promoted and moved out of the area) that ultimately resulted in a six-figure contract. The referring member did not find out about this until I mentioned it in a discussion. Our member never even received a "thank you" from the recipient of this introduction, much less found out what the referral led to.

ADVICE

I think the advice is obvious (if not, keep reading). Although the former member is no longer with us, I can assure you that his reputation suffered because of this lapse in common courtesy. One member developed a reputation for not returning phone calls. DON'T LET YOURSELF GET CAUGHT IN THIS TRAP. Your reputation is much like your credit rating. Once it's lost, it's tough to regain. And actually, it's easier to restore your credit rating than it is your reputation. Think about it.

We have come through five years of unprecedented economic times (at least since the Great Depression). Many of the old tricks that we used in the Old World will no longer work or at best are not as effective as they had been. Perhaps the old tricks still work, but because of competitive factors or other pressures, you are forced to find new marketing methodologies or skills.

DON'T BE AFRAID IF A FORMAL AND DISCIPLINED APPROACH TO NETWORKING IS NEW TO YOU.

EMBRACE NETWORKING. MAKE NETWORKING A PART OF YOUR DAILY ROUTINE. TAKE NETWORKING, AND TURN IT INTO A GAME.

NETWORKING IS ALL ABOUT RECOGNIZING THE OPPORTUNITY TO INTRODUCE TRUSTED PARTNERS INTO POTENTIAL REVENUE SITUATIONS.

YOU WILL SEE RESULTS OVER TIME.

Now that you've agreed that NETWORKING and our method will yield positive results for your business, it's time for you to start the formal process. The next chapters focus on some of the preliminary decisions you'll need to make as you lay the foundation for your *NETWORKING ROAD MAP*. You must first determine and set realistic expectations.

Highlights

- Networking is a journey. It's a process. It's a commitment.

- Successful networking will increase your revenue.

- You will have fun taking a formal and disciplined approach to networking.

- Build trust with your networking partners.

- Use networking to differentiate yourself and to increase brand awareness of not only your business but also you personally.

- Practice and use good listening skills.

- Recognize the individual power tools that good networking organizations offer members.

- Recognize that good, effective networking takes time.

- Be a Giver and not a Taker.

- Networking is about recognizing opportunities to introduce trusted partners into potential revenue situations and to make meaningful introductions.

- Two -

What Are Your Networking Expectations?

"Smart professionals who network with clear expectations always achieve success."

Jim Holmes
Sandler Sales Training
Nashville, TN

The *FIRST STEP* toward a pragmatic and effective approach to establishing a networking process is determining your expectations with respect to networking. In other words, **WHAT DO YOU WANT TO GET OUT OF IT?**

Yes, the obvious answer is "**OBTAIN MORE BUSINESS.**" But wait, you can reach other objectives (just as important) through networking.

It really goes deeper than just obtaining more business. You *MUST BE MORE SPECIFIC* about the various goals you have set for yourself. Every individual and each business are unique and will have different goals or hurdles that must be achieved or overcome. The networking process will assist you in some but not in others. It will be your job (with our assistance) to make sure that you are as efficient in this process as possible.

If you don't think through this process, the likely outcome will be disappointment, and you will not achieve whatever expectations you may have (typically from my experience, initial expectations are usually set too high and are unattainable). The end result is that you will quit the networking organization and walk away disappointed, having not met your initial expectations.

IT'S YOUR CHOICE: SUCCESS OR FAILURE.

STORY At the end of every year, I determine what percentages of my members have resigned from the Southeast Business Forums. In an organization like this, turnover is good and necessary. It really comes down to what level of turnover I'm comfortable with. I've determined that a turnover rate of 10% to 20% is acceptable. The next step is to determine why members resign. Usually, of the members who resign, somewhere between 90% and 95% will resign due to inactivity or lack of engagement in our process. Typically, I can predict who will resign with a high degree of accuracy (due to their low level of involvement).

ADVICE Do not consider joining a networking organization without a commitment to become involved beyond just attending the meetings. If you are not fully engaged in the process, you will not meet even the lowest goal you've set. You will waste your money and time. I tell potential members that if all they do is attend 100% of the meetings and that's it, I don't want their money. If they aren't engaged and proactive in the process we've established, they will fail to meet any expectation and ultimately will leave the organization.

HOW DO I DETERMINE MY EXPECTATIONS, LET ALONE SET EXPECTATIONS?

RULE #1: IF YOU DO NOT PUT SUFFICIENT TIME OR RESOURCES INTO A NETWORKING ORGANIZATION, YOU WILL NOT GET ANYTHING OUT OF IT.

Once you agree with RULE #1, you're 90% of the way toward becoming a **NETWORKING TOP PRODUCER**!

FIRST CONSIDERATION: Determine whether you are an introvert or an extrovert. Be honest with yourself. Believe it or not, I'm a "closet" introvert. I'm not comfortable working a room where I don't know anyone. SO YOU'RE NOT ALONE. There are more of us than of them.

SO YOU'RE AN INTROVERT. GET OVER IT AND CHANGE!

ADVICE Whenever I go to an event (whether I'm facilitating it or just attending), you know what I do? As soon as I open the car door and step out, I say out loud to myself, "IT'S SHOW TIME!" I put on my extrovert hat and get into a mindset that puts me into a networking mood.

SECOND CONSIDERATION: Determine your capacity for investing the necessary time to be successful. DO NOT OVEREXTEND YOURSELF ON

COMMITMENTS TO TOO MANY ORGANIZATIONS. Overextending will likely result in failure on all fronts. We will cover this in chapter 3.

ADVICE — Learn to say "NO" to avoid overcommitting yourself to too many organizations. If you overcommit, you lessen your chances of success in any of the organizations.

THIRD CONSIDERATION: Ask yourself what you want to get out of a particular organization. Each organization is different with respect to its motivations. You MUST make sure that your motivations match the motivations of the organization that you are considering joining. IF THESE DO NOT MATCH, YOUR EXPECTATIONS WILL NOT BE MET. So are you looking at an organization for social contacts? Do you want to develop relationships within your professional industry? Are referrals versus leads important to you? As you'll see in the next chapter, this is important so that you will be able to pick the appropriate organizations to join and then set expected results.

FOURTH CONSIDERATION: Take a look at the product or service you provide, and analyze the sales cycle. Certain services or products naturally lend themselves to obtaining more referrals than others. Short sales cycle services likely result in a higher number of referrals than say the very long sales cycle profession (e.g., wealth advisors or very specialized consultants).

If you come into a networking organization with the expectation that you will obtain one referral per month and your sales cycle is long, you will be disappointed. Likely, you will blame the organization when you set your expectations too high considering your sales cycle.

STORY — I have found that everyone falls on a Referral Continuum. For example, at one end of the continuum, someone selling document-copying machines is in a pure transactional industry. This will likely drive him to decide to join multiple networking organizations on all levels. However, on the other end of the continuum, a wealth advisor is purely relationship driven. She will likely join one or maybe two networking organizations, and they would need to be on a senior level. The seller of document-copying machines will likely receive a far greater number of referrals than the wealth advisor. The majority of us probably fall somewhere in the middle.

ADVICE — Determine where you fit on the Referral Continuum. Regardless of where your service or product fits, set your expectations low for the first year. Make your first expectation to get to know all members and what they do. Plan on going in as a Giver and not being a Taker. Potential referral partners will see right through you if you appear to be a Taker. Being a Giver will pay dividends as you immerse yourself in the networking process. I always thought it better for others to owe me than the other way around.

FIFTH CONSIDERATION: Ask yourself if you can easily describe your product or service. Services that can be easily understood by a third party will have a better chance of getting more referrals than services that are hard to understand. Look at it this way, *if I don't understand what you do, how will I be able to identify an opportunity to introduce you?*

STORY One of my former members is a consultant specializing in getting people to cooperate, specifically in a corporate setting. He had a very difficult time explaining to people (in a relatively condensed format) what he does. One day he complained to me that he had generated four or five referrals to another member, and he was upset that this member had not reciprocated. When I next saw the other member, I mentioned this conversation to him. His response was, "I've known this member now for three years and I still don't know what he does."

SO WHO'S AT FAULT HERE?

ADVICE While we will cover this in greater depth in a later chapter, you must develop a short description of what you do. We call this developing your "elevator speech." Your expectations and ultimate results will be tied directly to how well you get your message across to someone who can potentially introduce you into revenue situations. If you can't do this easily, it's your fault for not being able to convey the right message. If you have problems with this, find a friend who can help you condense and clarify your message.

SIXTH CONSIDERATION: Make sure that your motivating factors for joining match up with the organization's motivation. If you are strictly Business-to-Business, why would you join an organization that is predominantly filled with folks who operate on a Business-to-Consumer level?

STORY I can't tell you how many times I hear the story about how someone joined another networking group only to find out that she was sitting next to people who could never refer the type of business needed.

SEVENTH CONSIDERATION: Set pragmatic goals for your first year in the organization. You should be thinking in terms of getting to know your fellow members and what they do and how you can give back to the other members and the organization. Remember, it really only takes one booked piece of business to recoup your membership cost.

STORY One member was a young banker in town, but he knew a lot of people. He joined Southeast Business Forums. I saw him at the next six months of our monthly meetings, and I understood that he attended some but not all of the assigned Troikas (see below). After about six months, I noticed he stopped coming to the meetings. I found out that he was disappointed with the organization because he wasn't getting the referrals that he had expected by just showing up. This fellow had unrealistic expectations.

ADVICE Don't walk into a networking organization thinking that just because you show up you will be the recipient of referrals from others. This is especially true when the business model is built on developing relationships.

EXPECTATIONS ARE NOT MET BECAUSE THE PROPER HOMEWORK IS NOT COMPLETED.

DEFINITION A ***TROIKA*** is an assigned group of three members (or guests) who attend a monthly meeting of the Southeast Business Forums. It is the responsibility of those three individuals to get together between that meeting and the next monthly meeting for the purpose of getting to know each other on a deeper basis. This is done over coffee, breakfast, or lunch.

EIGHTH CONSIDERATION: Recognize that there are other ways you can expect to benefit from a networking organization besides getting referrals. How about the expectation of surrounding yourself with extremely competent professionals in hundreds of different business verticals and areas of expertise?

TOP-PRODUCING NETWORKERS UNDERSTAND HOW TO EFFECTIVELY USE THESE RESOURCES.

STORY When I was a commercial banker in Los Angeles, I actively and purposefully found ways to introduce my fellow members to my clients. I did this by finding out what problems my clients were having in their business outside of my area of expertise. Once I identified a tangible problem that I knew could be fixed easily, I introduced a fellow member to my client. That member would fix the problem expeditiously and professionally and *MOST IMPORTANT MAKE ME LOOK GOOD*. Once this happened, I became a value-added part of my client's team. It was an *EXCELLENT WAY TO DIFFERENTIATE MYSELF FROM MY COMPETITORS*.

STORY One of the natural by-products of a networking organization is that over time, the *TOP PRODUCERS* will develop a team of professionals (in different disciplines) around them so that when they go into a business engagement and find multiple problems, they have a trusted team of professionals right there to fix any problems. WHO WINS?

EVERYONE WINS!

ADVICE The stories above illustrate two examples of how you can use a networking organization to benefit you in other ways than just getting referrals. *YOU MUST THINK OUTSIDE THE BOX IN REGARD TO HOW YOU ARE GOING TO USE THE RESOURCES OF A NETWORKING ORGANIZATION.*

The act of booking new business through referrals is the *TANGIBLE BENEFIT* you receive; it can be quantified and measured. When you have a boss who must sign your expense report and thinks only in terms of ROI (Return on Investment), this is a no-brainer. Bankers are good at making those calculations.

However, when you use it for these other purposes, you are receiving an *INTANGIBLE BENEFIT*. This can become a problem when you must justify the membership cost to the boss who thinks like a banker (and has never had to step out into the sales world).

NINTH CONSIDERATION: Don't go into ANY networking organization thinking that you will like or get along with everyone or automatically become mutual referral sources with everyone in the group or organization. If you do, you'll increase the chances that you take the shotgun approach to networking, and that is *NOT THE MOST EFFICIENT WAY TO APPROACH THIS*.

ADVICE Go into any networking organization with the expectation that, over time, you will be lucky to find three or four solid referral partners.

TENTH CONSIDERATION: Don't expect everyone to be as good a networker as you are. Don't expect everyone to follow networking protocol as well as you do. Expect that over time you will develop a sense of who gets it and who doesn't.

ADVICE Just use your common sense. Once you've identified people of like mind, get to know them better. These are the people who understand and embrace networking. These are the relationships you want to nurture.

Now that you have mapped out what you expect to get out of a networking organization, it's time to determine which organizations are the best ones to ponder joining. This analysis is very important because it will determine whether you spend your money and time wisely. Remember there are only 168 hours in each week. After you deduct for sleep time, only 112 hours remain. You must be efficient in how you spend those hours.

Highlights

- What do you want to get out of it? It's your choice.

- You must commit yourself to the process; put the time into it to make the process work, and experience success.

- If you're an extrovert, you are at an advantage over the introvert. The introverts MUST force themselves to adapt.

- Don't overextend yourself for commitments to too many organizations. Learn to say, "NO."

- What characteristics do you expect to find in a networking organization?

- What is the sales cycle of your product or service? How does it fit into the style, culture, and business model of the organizations you are looking to join?

- Can you describe your product or service in a way that I'll remember you? If I don't understand what you do, how will I be able to identify an opportunity to introduce you?

- Make sure your motivation matches the motivations of the networking organization.

- Set pragmatic goals and expectations for that first year.

- Consider the other benefits with which a networking organization can assist in addition to creating the opportunity to give and get referrals. These are the intangible benefits.

- Three -

Which Networking Organizations Should I Join?

"In a networking group, it may take a while for the wheels to start turning, but don't waste your time if you feel the wheels spinning."

Mary-Michael Horowitz
Concept Technology, Inc.
Nashville, TN

THE **FIRST QUESTION** YOU ARE GOING TO ASK YOURSELF IS: "WHICH NETWORKING ORGANIZATION SHOULD I JOIN?"

THE **SECOND QUESTION** YOU ARE GOING TO ASK IS: "HOW MANY NETWORKING ORGANIZATIONS SHOULD I JOIN?"

I have no clue. It depends on a lot of factors, and those factors depend on you and your business. However, I think it's so important that you find the right one that I put this in the beginning of the book, and you'll find it to be the longest chapter.

HOW MUCH TIME DO YOU REALISTICALLY HAVE TO DEVOTE?

My experience is that this is the *SINGULAR* reason why people do not renew or return to a networking organization. In other words, they do not put the necessary time into making the process work.

Remember that unless you can put the right amount of time into making the networking process work, you will FAIL.

ADVICE Start with one networking organization that meets your criteria, and see how it goes. If you are an experienced networker, reevaluate the organizations you belong to with respect to the time you are able to devote compared to the return on your investment (time and money).

Remember that each organization has a different motivation and purpose. Some will require more of your time than others.

STORY The Southeast Business Forums business model is built on the philosophy of developing deep and long-lasting business relationships. It is strictly on a Business-to-Business basis. We believe that meaningful business referrals are generated through building solid relationships. It takes time for these relationships to develop so that a certain level of trust takes hold and you feel comfortable referring someone to your client.

ADVICE If you need to get that first solid referral in the first month and must book that first piece of business by the end of the month to keep your job, you are better off in a networking organization that is more transactional driven and specializes in leads versus referrals.

*You **MUST PRIORITIZE** what is important to you and the business. For some it is making contacts within your industry. Therefore a professional organization may be more important than a traditional networking group. Others may feel that a community-based group (e.g., Rotary or Kiwanis) is more important. If it is a Business-to-Business organization, what is the mix of business verticals in the organization and the group you are looking to join?*

ADVICE Start by analyzing the networking organization's business model. How is the model built? What is the general purpose of the organization? Are you pretty much on your own? Does the organization provide you with more than a monthly lunch or breakfast? What other services has the organization developed to assist you in your networking efforts? What are the value-added propositions that the organization brings to the table that will help you be successful in your networking efforts?

How many times does the organization meet? Typically it will be weekly or monthly. How many meetings per month can you realistically attend?

We've all heard that time is money, right? Well, it is. Personally, I'm comfortable with monthly meetings. When you're trying to juggle attendance at multiple events and still trying to get the work done that pays the bills, weekly meetings can be too much.

WHAT TYPES OF NETWORKING ORGANIZATIONS DO YOU HAVE TO CHOOSE FROM?

As you can see, when you start listing organizations in which you can network, there are so many that you don't realize you have at your fingertips. It's really a matter of prioritizing.

Traditional Networking Organizations
- Business-to-Consumer (B2C)
- Business-to-Business (B2B)
- Industry or business vertical specific
- Generalized business verticals
- Competition sensitive
- Quota requirements
- Attendance requirements
- Weekly or monthly meetings

Chambers of Commerce
- Member events
- Social interaction
- Mixture of B2B and B2C

Professional Industry Organizations
- Healthcare (e.g., Healthcare Council of Nashville)
- Marketing (e.g., Nashville American Marketing Association)
- Financial (e.g., Financial Executives International)
- Consulting (e.g., Turnaround Management Association)
- Legal (e.g., American Bar Association)
- Industry specific (e.g., Printing Industry Association)

Social Clubs
- City clubs (e.g., Nashville City Club)
- Country clubs
- Hobby clubs
- Fraternal clubs (e.g., Elks)

Church or Synagogue

Educational Organizations
- College alumni organizations
- Fraternity, sorority organizations

Community-Based Organizations
- Rotary
- Kiwanis
- Lions

Social Media
- LinkedIn groups
- Twitter

Each of these very different organization types has a different business model and motivation. Even though many organizations may fall into the same category, the organizations themselves may have different motivations, and their business models will not be the same.

WHAT ARE THE DEMOGRAPHICS OF YOUR CLIENT BASE?

You need to analyze who your clients are. What do they look like? As you look for the right networking organization, the probability of successful referrals (or any at all) will be significantly reduced if your client base doesn't match that of the average clients of the other networking members.

Who do you sell to?

Is your client base primarily consumer or business? If it's Business-to-Business, you are likely better off at a senior-level networking organization where the member emphasis is on Business-to-Business professionals.

What is the range of your clients' size (in revenue)?

Let's say that your target clients are large corporations with revenues of $500 million or more. You want to join a networking organization where the members typically target clients with revenues from $1 million to $25 million. Clearly there is a mismatch here, and the likelihood of your getting meaningful referrals into large corporations is very small. Your sandbox is not the same sandbox that the other members play in.

We lose several members each year because they are promoted within their company and their client base changes. They now are focusing on selling to larger companies. The Southeast Business Forums' typical member has a client base with annual revenues ranging from $1 million to $50 million. Once members begin targeting the "big" fish, there will be a mismatch between our organization and their prospect list. Naturally, they will seek other, better-suited organizations (or methods) to network.

Where are most of your clients located?

If your clients are not located in the town in which you live and you are constantly out of town visiting clients, you won't likely have the time to network effectively.

A C-Suite executive coach became a member because he wanted to do more business in Nashville. However, his client base was all over the country, and as a result, he was on an airplane all the time and didn't spend much time with his family. By joining the Business Forum, he thought he could expand his local business and spend more time in town. Well, the conundrum was that he was never in town to actively pursue the networking, and he never got any referrals. He quit.

ADVICE Make sure that if your motivation is to join a referral-based networking group, you determine the group's "sandbox" before you jump in and play. By the end of your first meeting, you will probably be able to figure it out after meeting the members and listening to their introductions. If you can't figure it out, ask the group leader directly.

HOW IS THE ORGANIZATION STRUCTURED?

You must determine whether the networking organization is structured from an individual-centric or a corporate-centric standpoint. What do I mean by this? Is the organization interested in signing you up as a corporate member or as an individual? I'm not trying to disparage either approach. However, for the type of networking culture that I believe in, the individual-centric approach is the better of the two. I don't really care about the company you work for because *YOU* are the most important part of the networking process. Companies don't network. *PEOPLE NETWORK*.

How are the meetings structured and run?

How many times have you gone into meetings at your company and become frustrated because they're run loosely and have no regard to staying on topic? In other words, don't you just love those four-hour meetings that could have been wrapped up in one hour? When you visit a networking meeting, does it start on time, and does it get you out at the time promised? A structured meeting with a defined agenda is a mark of a well-run networking organization, and that should be a plus when you consider joining the organization.

Are the agendas the same from meeting to meeting?

I happen to believe in the McDonald's Method. Regardless of which McDonald's you go into, you are assured of getting the hamburger and fries you expect. So the networking agenda is the same each month and at each chapter. My members know what to expect when they show up for a meeting, whether it's their chapter or one they are visiting. For a meeting with a defined purpose, structure is important.

How tightly controlled are the meetings?

Are the meetings run efficiently? Does the meeting leader have a sense of humor? Does he start the meetings on time and get you out when he says he will? How well does the group leader manage the group? Is there enough time built in so that members and guests can ask questions?

What are one or two aspects of the meetings or the structure of the meetings that are different from other networking organizations?

Networking organizations are different. They must differentiate themselves, just like your business must differentiate itself from the competition. Once you have identified your motivations and expectations, you will be able to recognize whether those differences between networking organizations match up with your specific needs.

Is the organization's purpose to have the best speaker each meeting, or is the purpose to provide its members with the environment for real networking and the results that go along with that?

Many organizations are speaker centric. In other words, these organizations rely on speakers to ensure attendance by their members. So basically, members make their decision to attend based on the speaker and/or the topic.

ADVICE

If the networking organization you are contemplating joining seems to be speaker centric, I would advise you to pass on it. The *PRIMARY* reason to go to your meetings is to connect with one or two key referral partners. I tell my members that *the reason you come to a Business Forum meeting is to be placed in a Troika*, not because of the speaker or topic that month.

Is competition allowed within each of the subgroups or chapters?

From a networking standpoint, I would not join an organization that allows competition among subgroups. There must be EXCLUSIVITY within the individual chapters. Most networking organizations have multiple groups or chapters, and competition is inevitable between chapters.

What is the guest policy?

Are guests welcomed only when they have a sponsoring member, or does the organization take in anyone who wants to attend (e.g., someone signs up on the website)? Are there certain responsibilities and expectations of the sponsoring members when it comes to their guest? A well-run formal networking organization will have some sort of vetting system process in place to ensure that a high quality of guests and members is maintained.

Is the organization consistent when scheduling its meetings?

Are the meetings held in the mornings, during the day, or at lunchtime? This factor affects your schedule or the way you bill. For example, attorneys bill by the hour, so we have found that early morning meetings are best for them since that time doesn't interfere with their billing hours.

How does the organization handle the situation when a guest wants to join, but there may be a competitive issue with a sitting member?

This is an important question to ask the group leader of any networking organization whose business model includes competitive exclusivity. There must be a defined process that protects the members, and they must be aware of it. It is a process that must be consistently applied. The policy should be structured so that a sitting member never feels threatened.

How does the organization view direct solicitation between its members and guests?

Many formal networking organizations do not address this issue. A nonsolicitation policy protects members from being put into uncomfortable situations that result from (e.g. the hard sell). This type of policy will protect the organization's reputation from what could be construed as predatory.

DEFINITION

NONSOLICITATION between members and guests means that no one can directly solicit business from another member or guest.

STORY

When I was a member of a senior-level networking organization in Los Angeles, another member asked if he could visit me at my office. No sooner had he stepped into my office than he started the hard sell on me. I kicked him out of my office, and bad feelings were a result. When I started the Business Forum, I remembered that situation and how it made me feel. So I created the "no direct solicitation" rule. I didn't want any of my members to be put in an awkward position.

ADVICE

I advise you to ask what position the organization takes with respect to direct solicitation between its members and guests. In a senior-level professional service provider organization, I think it's unprofessional to directly solicit another member's or guest's business.

Is the organization transparent?

At a minimum, find out who owns the organization. Is it a small business being run at the local level, a national organization, or perhaps even an international organization? Check the history of the organization for any red flags that might indicate trouble down the road.

STORY

Another networking organization pulled into town. I didn't know about it until someone called me to ask what I knew about it. As we all know, YOU MUST KNOW YOUR COMPETITION. I spent three hours on the computer researching this company. Loads of information were available. But I couldn't find out who owned this organization or how it was structured. You think this might be a red flag? Transparency is very important.

HOW ARE THE MEETINGS RUN?

The meeting is the first step. From an organizational standpoint, the meeting is the organization's elevator speech. It is the first impression that a guest will have. Who is the most important person in your business? I'll venture a guess that it isn't you. It's the first person that the client sees. When you walk into Williams & Sonoma, the floor salesperson will set the tone for future business. When you walk into a bank branch, it's the teller or new accounts representative. It's no different with the networking organization's meeting and the facilitator.

Who runs the meetings?

Make sure that you like the person who runs the meetings. Is it the same person for each meeting? He can make or break a meeting. He is also your contact for ensuring the process works for you. He should ALWAYS encourage you to ask questions, make suggestions for improvement, and let him know if there are problems.

Does the facilitator start the meetings on time and get you out on time as agreed?

Again, your time is money. Make sure the person running the meetings starts and ends on time. Does the program stay on track, or does the facilitator allow it to drift? A "loosey-goosey" run meeting is indicative of an organization without a road map.

Does the facilitator make your guests feel comfortable and welcome? Are premade name badges waiting for your guests?

Ever bring a guest to a meeting and have the host snub her? How did that make you feel? The little things distinguish well-run organizations from the ones that just make do. An example would be having premade guest name badges sitting alongside the members' name badges. Many organizations will have the guests fill out their own nametags. That may not be a big deal to some people, but to me, it is a small indicator of how a networking organization is run.

Is there variety in the agenda?

A monthly program can be constructed to provide variety while maintaining a consistent structure.

In the early years of the Southeast Business Forums, I structured the forty minutes of open time in our meetings with speakers. One day I got a call from a member who indicated that he wanted something more than just speakers (he felt he got enough of them through other organizations to which he belonged). So for the next several months I filled the forty minutes with "town hall" discussions on various topics. Then one day I got a call from another member who wanted to know why we didn't have speakers any longer. That's when I came to the realization that I couldn't please everyone. Now, I rotate between three formats: speaker, town hall discussion, or a program (facilitated by a member) with a theme based on a networking topic.

 Find out whether the regular meetings include a different program that changes from meeting to meeting. If that part of the program includes a member or two getting up each month and giving a commercial for themselves, STAY AWAY. That agenda is a recipe for failure. Why? Because first of all, not all members are good speakers, and you'll be bored in those situations. Second, not all members, because of time constraints, will be able to stand up and deliver that advertisement. When it's YOU that they pass over, how do you think you'll feel? Been there, done that.

How much "free" networking time do you get before and after the formal meeting?

A premeeting networking period should be thirty minutes. After the meeting has concluded there should be a period of time for networking so that the members can strategically seek out people they want to talk to.

How long are the meetings?

A ninety-minute meeting can accomplish everything that needs to be done provided the facilitator stays on task.

 I personally like meetings that are run tightly, whether it's networking, business, or otherwise. Sloppily run meetings are unprofessional and not worthy of my time. You should have that attitude when choosing the appropriate formal networking organization.

WHAT IS THE COST STRUCTURE FOR BELONGING?

Are you getting the value for your money? That is no different from anything else you buy. Good quality doesn't usually equal the cheapest product or service. Most of my members have the philosophy that if it's free, it isn't worth it.

What level is the organization?

Just like everything else, you get what you pay for. Yes, "speed networking" functions are relatively inexpensive compared to senior-level formal networking organizations. But what do you get for the time investment when you sit in front of someone for three minutes?

Does the organization charge only a one-time annual fee that covers ALL activities, or is it pay to play?

This is a matter of personal preference. I prefer an all-in, one-time payment that covers just about everything.

ADVICE Many networking organizations provide a cafeteria-style payment structure. In other words, you pay an annual fee, but they collect for each event (i.e., meeting costs). Make sure that when you are investigating a networking group, you ADD UP ALL of the costs (annual dues and all ancillary costs) to come up with your "all-in" annual cost. That is the only way you will be able to properly cost-compare multiple organizations.

What are the a la carte events, if any, that must be paid for outside the annual dues?

Ask what other events or services the organization offers its members that are not included in the annual dues.

Does the organization sponsor seminars or other events that come at a discount to members?

Are you on your own for these extracurricular activities, or does the organization contribute something for its members? Even though you may pay the annual dues that cover everything, the organization may believe that it is important to be a part of outside events. It may sponsor a table that its members are to fill. I don't think it's unreasonable for the members to pay in full or partially for their seats at the table. If nothing else, they have skin in the game and are more likely to show up (just the opinion of someone who has sprung for event tables and been stuck with empty seats).

Do guests pay for attending?

Some organizations collect money from guests at the door for the privilege of attending the normal meeting. Other organizations cover the cost of their guests. Which model do you think sends the best "vibes" to the guests and their sponsoring members?

HOW MANY OTHER CHAPTERS OR GROUPS DOES THE ORGANIZATION HAVE?

The more chapters or groups that networking organizations have mean more potential interaction among members. This is accomplished via interchapter visitation policies, all-chapter events, and other outside events sponsored by the networking organization where all members can participate.

Does the organization have multiple subgroups or individual chapters?

You can expand your network if the answer is yes.

Are you allowed to visit the other subgroups or chapters?

From a tactical standpoint, smart networkers take advantage of this. You need to ask about the visitation policy.

How many times are you allowed to visit other subgroups or chapters?

It may be unlimited, but usually you are limited to a certain number of visits per chapter or group during a calendar year.

Does the organization ever bring all of its members together for singular events that allow for interaction among members of different chapters?

Doing this gives the members a chance to network with members of other chapters and, in some ways, promotes a sense of belonging to the bigger organization as opposed to just an individual chapter or group.

ADVICE

Networking organizations that have multiple subgroups or chapters are more powerful for their members than "one-off" organizations. It's like compounding interest. The more visits you get, the more contacts you make.

WHO ARE THE MEMBERS OF THE ORGANIZATION?

Let's say you own an accounting firm and your practice specializes in doing taxes and audits for middle-market privately held companies with revenues exceeding $5 million. You decide to send your other partners out to begin their formal networking activities (you're tired of being the sole rainmaker for the firm). One of them visits a networking organization made up of plumbers, electricians, hairdressers, and well, you get my drift. Not that these folks are to be discounted, but they aren't in the target group.

How many members does the organization have? If you are looking at a specific subgroup or chapter to join, how many sitting members are there?

The more the merrier, as the slogan goes. Also ask about your competitors in the organization. If your line of business is the only one represented, you will be in the catbird seat, especially for visiting other chapters or groups.

What is the makeup of the membership from a diversification standpoint?

Yes, this encompasses gender and race. But it is also diversification of business verticals.

STORY

Without sacrificing membership quality, some of my goals for the Business Forum are to increase the membership of minorities and women. It's important to me that the Business Forum becomes known not as the "Best Women's Networking Organization" but as the "**Best Networking Organization for Women**." There's a big difference between the two.

What is the *QUALITY OF THE MEMBERS*?

To borrow a slogan from Ford Motor Company, "Quality is Job 1." If an organization is going to build its business model and culture around developing deep and long-lasting relationships, bringing in **QUALITY** members is crucial to the success of the organization and its members.

What are the business verticals represented by the members of the subgroup or chapter?

Ask how they determine the categories of members. You should be able to see the various verticals within the professional categories for members.

ADVICE Understand WHO the other members are and WHAT they are all about from a business standpoint. You want to ensure that your fellow members "fit into your space." One way to do this is take a look at the first circle of influence that surrounds your business. In other words, which business verticals are in the first orbit that have (or can have) direct synergy with you? Are these verticals represented in the networking organization?

DOES THE ORGANIZATION HAVE CERTAIN RULES THAT PROTECT MEMBERS?

Typically when you join a formal networking organization, you pay for certain things. One is that you and your seat should be protected within the chapter or subgroup. Another protection should be from "predatory" members (let's hope the culture and vetting process eliminate this from the start).

If the networking organization has a noncompetition policy, how is it enforced, and how are members protected within each group?

DEFINITION **NONCOMPETITION** or **EXCLUSIVITY** within a traditional networking organization is fairly standard and typically defined as any subgroup (i.e., chapter) allowing only one seat per business vertical, product, or specialty.

STORY The Southeast Business Forums business model is built on this exclusivity factor. Within each of our chapters, we try to ensure that there is no competition of its members. When someone expresses a desire to join, we look at two professional categories: primary and secondary. The primary professional category consists of thirteen verticals (e.g., banking, finance, marketing, consulting, etc.). The secondary category ultimately will determine whether a competitive issue exits. For example, there may be several bankers in one chapter, but that's okay since one banker may sit in the seat called "Senior Commercial Banker" while another banker sits in the "SBA Banker" seat. Competition is defined by the core product or service.

ADVICE Fully understand the "rules" of each networking organization when it comes to competition or exclusivity. While the organization will not likely offer its list of members, it should be able and willing to let you know the categories of its members.

Does the organization have a nonsolicitation policy between its members?

This was covered above. However, it's worth repeating. I can't tell you how many horror stories I've heard concerning predatory members pursuing other members or guests.

WHAT ARE THE ORGANIZATION'S EXPECTATIONS OF YOU AS A MEMBER?

If you don't understand what is expected of you, the folks running it and your fellow members may be disappointed in you.

Are there any quota requirements?

Quotas can refer to a minimum number of guests invited per month or quarter. It can also be part of a system of leads or referrals during a particular time period. If there are, be wary of the quality of referrals or leads.

Are you expected to bring guests?

Regardless of whether there is a quota system or not, I don't think this expectation is unreasonable. It is in the members' best interests to see the organization grow. Guests are the lifeblood of a networking organization.

Is there a minimum attendance requirement?

This is a no-brainer. If you're not willing or able to attend on a regular basis, don't join.

What are the organization's specific expectations of you?

Ask about expectations. Don't assume that you will be told up front.

 STORY You've probably already figured it out, but I don't believe in quota systems. My experience is that a quota system produces meaningless leads or referrals. Several of the top networking organizations in Los Angeles have quotas for their members. These typically are quarterly and involve a commitment for a minimum number of referrals and guests.

 STORY While the Southeast Business Forums has a guideline of 75% attendance, that is only one component of a member's ability to be successful. I tell prospective members that if they attend 100% of all meetings and the Troikas, but if that is all they do, I don't

STORY

want their check. Success in a networking organization is really based on a member being engaged and proactive in the process.

ADVICE

Any good networking organization should tell you that while you should expect to "receive," you should also expect to "give." These organizations seek prospective members who will add value to them over time. YOU MUST BE PROACTIVE AND ENGAGED IN THE ORGANIZATION'S PROCESS.

The Level of Your Involvement Will Define Your Success or Failure.

WHAT IS THE ENDGAME OF THE ORGANIZATION?

You should find out right away whether the networking organization is run like a health club or it really has your best interests at heart. In other words, is the primary motivation to just collect your check? If that's the endgame for them, whether you show up is going to be immaterial to the organization.

The Right Networking Organization for you is the one committed to ensuring you are provided with the right situations, opportunities, and products to increase the chances of more commerce coming your way.

Is your networking organization run like a health club, or is the endgame to increase commerce going back and forth between members?

A typical health club business model is to admit anyone and collect the checks. A large percentage of those members will fail to follow through on an attendance basis. But the club still has their money, and it goes to keeping the lights on.

Does the organization regularly weed out members who do not participate?

Doing this ensures that only the active and engaged members remain in the organization. I'm always asked about our turnover rate like that's a bad thing. Turnover in a networking organization is a good thing. What really has to be analyzed is a comfortable level of turnover. If turnover goes over a certain percentage (excluding one-time pressures, such as price increases), the organization needs to look inward and start asking itself hard questions.

STORY

Every year I "handicap" the membership from the standpoint of who I think will renew or not renew membership. I always have a very high percentage of being correct. Why? Because I know who is active and who is not. Usually, those members resign on their own, but sometimes I have to help them along.

Does the organization follow through with members who violate its rules?

Rules violators MUST BE dealt with immediately. Why? It's not fair to the other members if problems aren't addressed quickly.

Is the organization always looking for ways to ADD VALUE for its members? Does it add new products or services to enhance members' experience? Does the organization, like any business, continuously evolve?

A good networking organization is no different from any business, including yours. Unless the organization continues to add value to your membership, why stay? I believe this should go beyond providing a room for a meeting and a meal.

Is there an alternative agenda hidden within the organization?

Not sure I've ever personally run into or been aware of this with any of the networking organizations that I've been associated with. No, wait. I started the Nashville Business Forum for the sole purpose of getting commercial banking referrals. My bad.

Southeast Business Forums is a traditional networking organization, and its sole purpose is to assist in the creation of commerce among its members. We are not a political or religious organization. Therefore we do not allow issues other than business and networking to creep into our agenda. On occasion, I will sponsor tables at a local university's quarterly Business Breakfasts. At one of the breakfast meetings, the speaker was the head coach of the Tennessee Titans. Several of my members asked me why I didn't sponsor a table for this particular breakfast. I had to respond that while one could argue this event was about networking, the fact is the Business Forum is about business and not professional football. The other three breakfast meetings with such keynote speakers as the heads of Opryland and Genesco Corp. and the mayor of Nashville were well received by my members.

Ask existing members (perhaps start with your sponsor) about whether the organization does a good job of staying in tune with its members and adding value.

Three: Which Networking Organizations Should I Join?

Highlights

- How much time do you have to devote to networking? Be honest with yourself.

- What type of organization should you join? There are lots out there to choose from, but only a few will accomplish what you wish to achieve.

- You must determine the demographics of your client base so as to ensure you match up with the appropriate networking organization.

- Look at how the networking organization is structured. Does it meet your expectations?

- How are the regular meetings run; tightly or loosey-goosey?

- What is the cost structure? Are you getting the most for your dollar?

- Does the organization protect its members with policies for exclusivity (i.e., competition) and nonsolicitation (i.e., no direct solicitation between members and guests)?

- Who are the sitting members of the organization you're thinking of joining, and what business verticals are represented? Is it the right match for you and your business?

- Do you have a problem living up to the expectations that the organization may have of you?

- Can you determine the endgame of the organization you are contemplating joining?

- Four -

Networking Protocol

"Not setting a protocol for networking with others can create a disaster; not following a protocol you've set with others creates distrust."

Tim Stowell
Cresa Nashville
Nashville, TN

Have you ever considered what happens when your credit rating takes a hit? You won't be able to buy that new car at the best interest rate reserved for clients with excellent credit. Some vendors won't do business with you (other than on a cash-only basis).

The worst thing that can happen to someone's credit rating is filing for personal bankruptcy (corporate bankruptcy has become a strategy and is no longer a stigma). In the old days, it took seven years for the bankruptcy to clear off someone's record.

IT'S EVEN WORSE WHEN YOUR REPUTATION TAKES A HIT.

Believe it or not, it's *HARDER* to clear your reputation than it is to clear your credit rating.

You strive very hard to build and maintain a good reputation in your industry, with your clients and your vendors. There is a popular saying that goes like this:

Your Reputation Is Everything.

THAT HOLDS TRUE WHEN YOU NETWORK.

YOU MUST BUILD AND MAINTAIN A GOOD REPUTATION WITH YOUR NETWORKING PARTNERS.

HOW DO YOU BUILD AND MAINTAIN A GOOD REPUTATION WITH YOUR NETWORKING PARTNERS?

It's easy. It's common sense. It's a process. And it's called

"THE GOLDEN RULE"

We all know that not everyone is the same. All of us were mentored differently. But when the day is done, we all want to be treated as we hope we treat others.

Networking protocol can be learned. It really is a process and should be embedded within your daily networking habits.

These protocol suggestions are generic and, as you will see, can be handled in multiple ways, depending on your preference. The important thing to remember is that *YOU MUST FOLLOW THESE IF YOU WANT TO MAXIMIZE YOUR NETWORKING EFFORTS.*

THERE IS ONLY *DOWNSIDE* FOR YOU IF YOU DO NOT FOLLOW PROPER PROTOCOL.

PEOPLE WHO ARE GOING TO HELP YOU THE MOST ARE GOOD NETWORKERS, AND THEY UNDERSTAND AND PRACTICE THESE PROTOCOLS.

THEY WILL EXPECT YOU TO DO THE SAME!

DEFINITION

A REFERRAL is an introduction for an individual into a potential piece of business. This is typically considered a warm referral in which a problem has been identified, and the referring partner will build your credibility with the prospect.

AN INTRODUCTION is introducing two people that you think should get together for a discussion, typically on a common interest.

A LEAD is someone saying, "Hey, you should call this company." No real thought has been given to the purpose or that the referring person even knows anyone in the company.

This is one of those things that everyone learns in kindergarten but sometimes forgets: "THANK YOU."

If you do nothing else, remember this.

I'm always dismayed when I hear about someone who is not thanked for a referral. I make a mental note of that for the future.

In the old days, a handwritten note was offered up. Today, each of us has a different way of handling the "thank you" for a referral or an introduction.

- *Verbal*: this is the bare minimum. Ideally, this should be combined with one of the others below.

- *E-mail*: alone, it seems very cold. Pair it up with one of the others, and you're good to go.

- *Handwritten*: very classy now that most people don't write thank-you cards any longer. It will definitely set you apart.

- *Testimonial*: verbal and written—see ADVICE below.

- *Gift*: a bottle of wine for a referral that got booked?

- *Dinner*: for a BIG REFERRAL THAT GOT BOOKED!

- *Trip to Paris*: I've never seen this done.

ADVICE I think one of the most powerful "thank you" strategies is to give both a verbal and a written testimonial to the referral source. At a minimum, you would be expected to give a verbal acknowledgment at your next regular networking meeting. If you are a LinkedIn user, a post on LinkedIn goes a long way (you don't have to get into the details of the deal).

You should NEVER make ASSUMPTIONS.

If you give a referral or if you are on the receiving end of a referral, make sure each of you knows the other's expectations with respect to how the process should proceed. Everyone has a different set of expectations.

DON'T ASSUME WHAT YOU THINK IS AN ADEQUATE PROCESS IS THE OTHER PERSON'S IDEA OF ADEQUACY.

For some people, FOLLOW-UP is the most important part of the process.

THIS PERTAINS TO BUSINESS REFERRALS AS WELL AS INTRODUCTIONS.

Remember, you are likely being referred to your referral source's client. There is a strong chance that your referral source wants to be kept up to date with how things are going. No one likes surprises, especially bad ones.

Even if the referral or introduction doesn't involve the referral source's client, it is necessary for you to ask your referral source how much feedback she expects to get. At the very least, an acknowledgment of the introduction is necessary.

I happen to try (although we don't always succeed, do we?) to give some feedback to my referral source regardless of whether he tells me it's not necessary. Many times, people will tell you that it doesn't matter. However, I've found in many circumstances that it does matter to them despite what they say. So just make it part of your process to follow up.

Basic referral feedback includes the following:

Acknowledgment to your referral source of the referral with a *"thank you."* I can't overemphasize this enough. You may think that this is automatic. Let me tell you that too many people never utter those two simple words.

Acknowledgment to your referral source of making contact (or making the attempt) with the person to whom he referred you or introduced you. It's likely that unless you tell your referral source that contact has been made, he won't hear about it, and you will get a phone call from him. Don't let that happen.

If you run into any *problems*, it is best to let your referral source know immediately. Remember, there are always two sides to every story, and *you want to make sure that your story is heard first.*

At the conclusion of your business with the client, let your referral source know *what transpired.*

BOTTOM LINE: REMEMBER THAT NO ONE EVER WANTS TO BE SURPRISED.

ADVICE

I recommend that you ask your referral source at the time he makes the referral or introduction. A simple "How much feedback do you want?" is all you need to elicit the discussion.

How do you make an effective REFERRAL?

The first criterion for making an effective referral is understanding your client's problem and then matching it to the person who has the right skills to fix it. If you do this properly, *YOU WILL LOOK GOOD TO YOUR CLIENT.*

A personal introduction might be warranted here. It's your call as the referring partner and whether circumstances (e.g., client, distance, timing, etc.) will dictate the direction you go.

Building up your referral partner to your client will help establish her credibility and go a long way toward helping her win the business.

If you are being referred into a potential business situation, it is your responsibility at some point to say really good things about your referral source. *That's quid pro quo.*

BUSINESS IS NOT WON UNLESS A PROBLEM CAN BE FIXED.

How do you make an effective INTRODUCTION?

Like the method of "Thank You," there are multiple ways to make an introduction. It really boils down to your choice and circumstances.

At a minimum, you are going to give someone a slip of paper with the contact information. Frankly, to me this is nothing more than a lead. When someone does that to me, I think, *Heck, I could just look in the Yellow Pages and make a cold call on someone for what this is worth.*

At the other end of the spectrum, I've got some members who won't make introductions unless they can do it in person. That's an admirable approach; however, it may not be practical in most circumstances.

I'm comfortable with an e-mail introduction as long as it is structured properly, contains the information needed for the parties to connect, and has a purpose behind it.

ADVICE The Appendix has an example of the type of e-mail that I send to all parties when I make the introductions.

Your *INTRODUCTION SHOULD MAKE SENSE* to both parties. Think about why you are introducing them. Be sensitive to their time. You'll see in a moment what happens when one party views the introduction as a waste of time.

If you're not sure whether both parties view the introduction as important as you do, contact each of them separately to make that determination. Better to do your homework up front rather than risk being put in an embarrassing situation.

What's the BIGGEST MISTAKE you can make when contemplating introducing people to each other?

IT'S MAKING AN INTRODUCTION THAT HAS NO MEANING.

STORY I hadn't really given this any thought until a member approached me and complained (I don't take these discussions as complaints; they are suggestions for improvement) that he was being introduced by other members to people who had no relevancy to his business. He met with them out of courtesy, but as he put it to me, "I bill by the hour, and these meaningless introductions cost me money."

Four: Networking Protocol

ADVICE Before you make an introduction, think about why you are connecting these two people. In your formal introduction, outline the reason(s) for making the connection so each party is aware up front of the agenda. Be sensitive to others' time.

What's the most important thing you can do when you are making a referral?

YOU CAN ESTABLISH THE CREDIBILITY OF THE PERSON YOU ARE REFERRING TO THAT SPECIAL CLIENT OF YOURS.

How do YOU structure that first sales call? You don't know the person you're sitting in front of so you must find something to bond with him and at the same time establish your credibility.

Well, let me tell you that your sales call will immediately become much more efficient if you allow someone else to establish your credibility. That "someone" should be the person who refers you into that opportunity.

ADVICE One of the more powerful aspects of belonging to a strong networking organization is that your fellow members know that one of their responsibilities of being the referral partner is to build credibility for the person they refer into the opportunity.

What are the expectations you must live up to when being referred into an opportunity?

You should reinforce with the client why she is lucky to have the relationship with the person who referred you. This is only fair, don't you think? It's another quid pro quo.

You must keep your referral partner informed. Communication should be a priority.

You are expected to return phone calls (yes, I know this seems pretty basic, but do you know how often I hear complaints about folks not returning phone calls or e-mails in a timely manner?).

If you run into problems, let your referring partner know as soon as possible.

Make your referral partner look good. Fix the client's problem efficiently and professionally. The best outcome is for the client to see your referral partner as a value-added member of the management team.

Once the engagement is completed, a personal "Thank You" and testimonial (verbal and/or written) are expected.

What about confrontation?

We will discuss CONFRONTATION in greater detail in chapter 8. Confrontation can be used as a tactic in networking if used properly.

However, from a protocol standpoint, confrontation is okay. I'm not talking about an "in your face" confrontational situation. It can be done in a nonthreatening way. I think that it's okay to let someone know that expectations have not been met.

During a portion of our chapter meetings time is reserved for our members (and guests) to stand up and thank others for referrals, introductions, and even booked business. I'm dismayed when I hear about people not verbally acknowledging others. Yes, I even forget from time to time to thank people. But what I tell everyone is that if I miss thanking him or her, tell me. My reaction will be to apologize, but I will make it a point to acknowledge them at the next meeting. I owe it to them.

What about quotas and reciprocal expectations?

A quick discussion on the quid pro quo of referrals is necessary. I've already mentioned that I don't like formal quotas. When people are forced to come up with leads or referrals just to satisfy an artificial quota, over time they will tend to reach for those leads. The result usually tends to be leads or referrals that have no teeth to them. It will ultimately lead to a not-so-good reputation on the part of the referring partner.

However, I do believe that you must *KEEP SCORE* in a culture of formal networking. Create a compartment in your brain called "Network Score Card." While it's an informal process, you will not be as efficient as you could be if you don't do this as part of your networking process.

I have found that the idea of keeping score is one of the more hotly contested opinions. Some favor it (I do), and others don't. Why would I continue to refer to someone who doesn't reciprocate? To me, it doesn't make sense. There are only 168 hours in a week (112 hours after you subtract time to sleep), and I have to make the best use of those hours. I'd rather spend them on referral partners who send me business.

I met with a member to discuss how he could be more efficient in his networking activities. He mentioned that he had given nine referrals to an attorney over the past year (not a member of the Business Forum). He indicated that all nine referrals resulted in booked business for the attorney. I naturally asked my member how many reciprocal referrals he had received from the attorney. None, he answered. My member never approached this attorney to find out why he never reciprocated. As I pointed out to my member:

YOU MISSED AN OPPORTUNITY!

I figured out that it was an issue of CONFRONTATION (see above) that kept my member from discussing this situation.

 Not all people believe in keeping score. There is a difference in keeping score with respect to networking versus connecting (i.e., the act of introducing). In chapter ten I discuss becoming a Connector: keeping score as a Connector will only lead to frustration. I respect the reasons given for not following this advice. However, my experiences have been very positive when I have kept score and held referral partners accountable. As you will see later on, if you don't keep score, how will you know to move people up and down in your Network Matrix? If you don't keep score, you will miss revenue opportunities.

BE SENSITIVE TO OTHER MEMBERS.

As a member of a networking organization, you may be given the opportunity to stand up and give testimonials at regular meetings. Although these testimonials are very powerful, they can backfire if you're not careful.

Let me give you an example. Your meetings will likely have guests who might compete with sitting members. I have seen members give glowing testimonials to those guests while their fellow members are in attendance. It is usually something that doesn't cross our members' radar until it's pointed out to them that it puts the sitting member in an uncomfortable position. Anyway, just something to think about.

 Have you ever gone to a restaurant and had a terrible experience? Sure you have. Everyone has. What happens next? It's likely that you'll never go back. It's also likely that you will not tell the owner why you're not coming back. However, you will tell all your friends why you're never going to eat at that restaurant again.

 If your referral partner has a bad experience with you, I can guarantee that not only will you never get another referral or introduction from this person but also he or she will make sure that other members of the networking organization know about that experience with you.

This Is Your Reputation That You Must Protect.

Highlights

- Your reputation is everything! Work at building and maintaining a good reputation with your referral partners.

- You start with a simple "Thank You" (verbal, e-mail, handwritten, and/or testimonials).

- Set expectations with your referral partner.

- Regardless of what your referral partner says, keep him or her informed. No one likes a surprise, especially from a client.

- If you're the referring partner, ask how your partner would like to be introduced (in person, e-mail, conference call, etc).

- Don't make an introduction that has no meaning to either party.

- Establish the credibility of the person you're referring into that special opportunity.

- As the person being referred into that special situation, you have a responsibility to reciprocate and build up your referral partner in the eyes of her client.

- Confrontation is okay if handled properly with respect.

- Keep score. If you don't, you are likely to miss opportunities.

- Five -

Reaching the Nirvana of Networking

"When you find yourself talking to someone and instead of thinking about yourself, you think of someone you know who needs to meet this person, you've reached the Nirvana of networking."

Stewart Ross
Southeast Business Forums, LLC
Nashville, TN

I believe in the **ONE PERCENTERS**.

No, I'm not referring to the patch that the Hells Angels members wear on the sleeve of their colors (how many of you know that story?).

I'm referring to the people who represent the best of their industry or the top 1%. The other 99% are ordinary and do just enough to get by. You know instantly who they are when you meet them.

The *ONE PERCENTERS* are the folks who always seem to be the consistent top producers in their organizations. They are the business owners who stay on the cutting edge of their industry. They are the businesspeople who can adapt and survive in the worst business environments. They are the businesspeople who stay ahead of the curve. They are the professional service providers who put the clients' needs ahead of their own.

STORY

I'm fond of telling people, "You've reached the Nirvana of networking when you can identify opportunities for others by asking questions outside your area of expertise."

Your Goal Is To Reach The Nirvana Of Networking.

ADVICE

When you look at the members of the Southeast Business Forums or any networking organization who are at the top of their game, they are all professionals who have climbed that hill and reached the Nirvana of networking.

How do you know that you've reached the NIRVANA of NETWORKING?

You have taught yourself to sit in front of someone and ask questions that can identify potential opportunities for a referral partner.

We are all very good at asking questions of our clients and prospective clients to identify ways we can assist (and ultimately make some money). I believe in traditional selling theory. This is called "asking probing questions."

Try to begin asking questions outside your area of expertise so as to identify those opportunities to introduce a referral partner. When I was a banker, I would ask a client, "Give me two or three examples of some issues you are facing in areas outside of our banking relationship. Perhaps I may be able to assist you through my contacts."

I would always be provided with examples. My clients weren't stupid. Why turn down an opportunity for free advice and perhaps solve problems?

You have taught yourself how to convey what you do in a concise and easily understood way.

You are able to make a potential referral partner remember what you do. If he doesn't remember you, he won't be able to remember to introduce you. It's that simple.

You are able to leave someone with a simple question she can ask in order to identify a potential opportunity to refer you into.

Give people something they can put into one of those little compartments in their brains that they can pull out at the right time.

You have taught yourself to be a good listener.

You can't remember anything if you don't listen well. Every professional sales trainer I've heard says the most successful sales call is when the prospect talks the entire time (or conversely, when *you* don't talk). The next chapter will continue our discussion on reinforcing how proper networking skills will result in greater revenue.

- Always look your conversation partner in the eyes.

- Don't interrupt.

- Wait for him to finish his thought (not just the sentence) before you talk.

- Don't race forward in your mind; you will not hear or compartmentalize what she is saying.

- Develop a follow-up question or statement while the other person is talking but don't develop multiple ones. Doing that just junks up your brain, and again, you won't really be listening to what he says.

- Concentrate on your conversation partner.

You have developed the ability to compartmentalize your brain.

I haven't figured out whether this is just something you're born with or whether you can actually train yourself to do this. If you can successfully juggle fifty tasks at one time, moving from one project to another and back again without missing a beat, I suspect you have a compartmentalized brain.

Several of President Bill Clinton's attributes were (are) his photographic mind and the ability to compartmentalize issues and move effortlessly from one to another. It is a rather unique talent.

You have reached a new comfort level in networking.

What was once something you shied away from is now a new comfort zone for you.

- Your comfort zone was pushing paper all day long. Picking up the telephone to make cold calls gave you the cold sweats.

- For one reason or another, you're forced to pick up the telephone and make cold calls. You start enjoying it. You make a daily game of it.

- All of a sudden, you no longer want to push paper because the process of bringing in new business is more enjoyable. You now look for ways to get someone else to process that paperwork.

YOU'VE REACHED YOUR NEW COMFORT ZONE.

You have reached a level of confidence in your networking skills.

Networking has started to become second nature to you. You are enjoying the process. You are starting to see success as a result of your networking efforts, and that just fuels the networking engine.

- You are actively looking for ways to introduce people.

- You are keeping an informal quota system based on referrals.

- You are confident enough to ask someone why she doesn't reciprocate when you've given her multiple referrals and you've gotten zippo, nada, the big donut.

- You've learned how to approach people on a nonconfrontational basis to ask them why they shun you.

- You aren't afraid to move on from someone who doesn't seem to understand the process you are trying to share with him.

- You are constantly elevating and demoting referral partners on your networking spectrum, depending on their activities with you.

- You are confident in your abilities to identify potential referral partners and not waste your time with folks who will never fit that bill.

- You've developed the delicate balance between networking activities and actually getting the real job done.

I've found it difficult to train people to be good networkers unless they have the seeds within their DNA for it. It's like good customer service. I can teach you how to answer the telephone, but I can't teach you excellent customer service skills. It's built into you, or it's not. The Ritz Carlton hotel knows this.

The Great Recession has forced a lot of people out of the protective corporate womb. They must now become consultants, and quickly they realize that one of those many hats they wear is marketing their products or services.

You can take those networking skills you have and build on them. This chapter has examined some of those traits that will elevate someone's skills to the next level. The next chapter will continue our discussion on reinforcing how proper networking skills will result in greater revenue.

Highlights

- Teach yourself to ask questions of your clients outside your area of expertise. These discussions will reveal opportunities for you to make introductions to your referral partners.

- Teach yourself how to frame what you do in a concise and easily understood way.

- Teach yourself to be a good listener.

- Develop an ability to compartmentalize your brain so that you can juggle multiple tasks and move effortlessly between them without dropping any of the balls.

- Reach what we call the "Networking Comfort Zone" or the "Nirvana of Networking."

- Six -

Social Capital and Social Competence

"Social capital's value is measured not in the number of contacts, clicks, hits, likes or friends, but the mutual goodwill fostered through personal relationships sustained over time."

Stan York
Belmont University
Nashville, TN

Why did I include a chapter on social capital and social competence? These two theories are closely linked to the fabric called networking. Although the consensus seems to be that social capital is very difficult to measure in quantitative terms, I believe that if people are socially competent, they will be better networkers (and connectors) and will ultimately increase their business. I see it happen day in and day out in my role of running the Southeast Business Forums.

This chapter is NOT intended to be a theoretical discussion along the lines you would pick up in a sociology course in college. It is meant to be a validation of my premise that you will make more money if you embrace and practice a formal and disciplined approach to networking.

What Is Social Capital?

SOCIAL CAPITAL = ACCESS TO OPPORTUNITIES

High Levels of Social Capital = Better Teamwork = Better Ability to Exploit Opportunities = Higher Levels of Revenue

DEFINITION

"Social capital is the expected collective or economic benefits derived from the preferential treatment and cooperation between individuals and groups." (Wikipedia)

"An economic idea that refers to the connections between individuals and entities that can be economically valuable. Social networks that include people who trust and assist each other can be a powerful asset." (Investopedia)

"The commonalities of most definitions of social capital are that they focus on social relations that have productive benefits." (Tristan Claridge, "Definitions of Social Capital," *Social Capital Research*, January 7, 2004)

"Through their social network, it is the 'goodwill available to individuals or groups,' and is expressed in the form of: gratitude, reciprocity, respect, and friendship. It is the accumulation of resources that you develop through networks and relationships that can help you flourish." (Carl DeVilbiss, Cooproductive)

"Social capital is a collective mental disposition close to the spirit of community." (Social Capital Foundation)

Tristan Claridge points out in his article "Definitions of Social Capital" that there are many disagreements about the definition of *social capital*. Nevertheless, as you can see from the quotations above, there is a clear singular theme about social capital, and that is SOCIAL CAPITAL IS ECONOMICALLY VALUABLE.

WHAT ARE THE BENEFITS OF SOCIAL CAPITAL?

1. **Information:** Gaining opportunities, trends, developments, etc.
2. **Influence:** Gaining access, establishing credibility, reputation, etc.
3. **Collective:** Action sharing interests, building trust.
4. **Bonding:** Developing long-term relationships.
5. **Bridging:** Connecting.

ARE THERE POTENTIAL NEGATIVES ASSOCIATED WITH SOCIAL CAPITAL?

Yes, and I point them out so you can do your best to avoid them and make your social capital experience a better one by recognizing some of the potholes.

- Social capital is not equally available to all. (Wikipedia)
- Social capital is not always created equally.
- There is the potential for the exclusion of outsiders.
- It could lead to excess claims on group members.

WHAT ARE SOCIAL CAPITAL MOTIVES?

According to many sources, there are four basic motivations. The underlying important factor is SELFISHNESS. Basically, you make a decision on how to allocate your resources (i.e., time and money) to create positive "goods" for yourself based on your relationships with others.

1. Feeling validated by acting consistently with the values of one's ideal self.
2. Feeling validated by others by winning their approval.
3. Seeking to belong.
4. Recognizing your sympathy or social capital for another person will motivate you to act in his or her interest.

What Is Social Competence?

SOCIAL COMPETENCE = INCREASED CHANCE FOR SUCCESS

High Level of Social Competence = Greater Financial Success

A higher level of social competence will result in the ability to establish and manage relationships that are healthy and productive for both parties.

Someone who has reached a higher level of social competence will exhibit the following skills:

- **Social perception**: Accuracy in perceiving others (i.e., traits, intentions, motives, etc.).
- **Impression management**: A wide range of techniques for inducing positive reactions in others.

- **Persuasiveness**: Ability to change others' views or behaviors in face-to-face encounters.

- **Social Adaptability**: Ability to adapt to, feel comfortable in a wide range of social situations.

- **Expressiveness**: Ability to express one's emotions and feelings clearly in productive ways to generate enthusiasm in others.

- Providing training in social competence skills might assist in entrepreneurs' ability to exploit opportunities and establish successful ventures (ever notice how teams of entrepreneurs tend to find MORE new ventures?). This could also be classified as social mentoring skills.

WHAT ARE THE THREE DIMENSIONS OF SOCIAL CAPITAL?

STRUCTURAL: this is one's network of overall pattern of connections. Strong network relationships require more effort and intimacy, which are more difficult to create and maintain. You will have fewer of them.

RELATIONAL: this is the strength of relationships, which includes time, emotional intensity, trust, intimacy, reciprocal services, etc. It is trusting that others will behave or perform or deliver that can motivate individuals to seek opportunities and act on them.

COGNITIVE: this is the shared vocabulary, representations, and interpretations. Social capital is derived from being embedded in a network and shapes the entrepreneur's cognitive processes and ultimately behavior. Shared meanings and understandings can act as a bonding mechanism that allows members to feel comfortable sharing resources and knowledge.

WHAT ARE YOUR SOCIAL CAPITAL RESOURCES?

- Contacts
- Information
- New opportunities
- Reputation and presence
- Knowledge
- Ideas
- Referrals and positive word of mouth
- Testimonials
- Reciprocal action

SPECIFIC ACTION STEPS TO BUILD SOCIAL CAPITAL

- Always be very dependable and professional.

- Always be on time.

- Always treat people with respect, care, and dignity.

- Demonstrate a great attention to detail.

- Provide a high level of customer service.

- Be there for other individuals when they need a sounding board or want your opinion on one thing or another.

- Always hand out referrals for people in need of services or products that you may not be able to provide.

- Give your clients a personal call. Ask about the last project you did, and ask if there's anything else you can do to help.

- Call all the people who have referred business to you. Ask how things are going: try to learn more about them and their activities so you can refer business or make introductions to them.

- List fifty people to stay in touch with (anyone who's given you business or introductions in the past twelve months and other prospects you've connected with recently). Send your key referral partners a birthday card each year.

- Follow up. Send a handwritten card after receiving a referral or any significant event.

NETWORKING AND SOCIAL CAPITAL ARE A JOURNEY.

Let's go back to my earlier comments about how many of us are naturally introverted, and it's tough for us to work that room when we don't know everyone. Many leaders you'll run across are shy. I've worked for a lot of bankers who were very smart with a balance sheet. I'm sure many of them probably followed the advice written in the book *The Seven Things That Make People Successful.*

What they should be reading is Jeff Haden's "*6 Habits of Remarkably Likable People*" (*Inc.*, January 2, 2013). Here's what he has to say about "getting people to genuinely like you." Mr. Haden states, "When you meet someone, after, 'What do you do?' you're out of things to say. You suck at small talk, and those first five minutes are tough because you're a little shy and a little insecure." *(Stew's Note: Over the years, I've read or been told that one common trait shared by many business leaders is their personal insecurity.)*

How do you make a good impression in little time?

LOSE THE POWER POSE.

Don't try to establish your importance through nonverbal self-confidence. Remember, you want the interaction to be more about them than about you. They will remember you if you turn the conversation toward them. People like to talk about themselves.

- Talk normally; don't crush the person's hand when you shake it.

- Step forward with a smile and bend slightly forward as if, ever so slightly, to bow. (You put aside all sense of self-importance or status. You will be seen as genuine.)

- Relax and show that you're the one honored by the introduction.

- Be genuine. We all like people who like us. If I show you I'm genuinely happy to meet you, you'll instantly start to like me.

	TAKE	**GIVE**
Strategy:	Competitive	Cooperative
Attention:	Inward	Outward
Feeling:	Anxiety/Wary	Acceptance
Action:	Take	Give/Receive
Source:	Mind	Heart
State:	Tense	Relaxed
Orientation:	Risk/Lack	Reward/Plenty
Awareness:	Unconscious	Conscious

EMBRACE THE POWER OF TOUCH.

Nonsexual touch can be very powerful. Touch can influence behavior. *(Stew's Note: I've read somewhere that wait staff at restaurants are taught to lightly touch the client because it has been shown that the touch results in higher tips.)*

Go easy, of course. Pat the other person lightly on the upper arm or shoulder. Make it casual and nonthreatening. Mr. Haden points out Bill Clinton's gestures when he meets Nelson Mandela. It comes across as genuine and sincere.

Touch breaks down natural barriers and decreases the real and perceived distance between you and the other person; touch is a key component in liking and in being liked.

WHIP OUT YOUR SOCIAL JIU-JITSU.

(Stew's Note: This is a good one. This comes from Mr. Haden's article.)

You meet someone. You talk for fifteen minutes. You walk away thinking, "Wow, we just had a great conversation. She is awesome."

Then, when you think about it later, you realize you didn't learn a thing about the other person.

Likable people are masters at Social Jiu-Jitsu, the ancient art of getting you to talk about yourself without you ever knowing it happened. SJJ masters are fascinated by everything you say.

SJJ masters use their interest, their politeness, and their social graces to cast an immediate spell on you. *(Stew's Note: I'm sure that each of us can name at least one person we know who fits the SJJ master title.)*

No one gets too much recognition. Asking the right questions implicitly shows you respect another person's opinion and by extension, the person.

WHIP OUT SOMETHING GENUINE.

Everyone is better than you at something. Let others be better than you.

Too many people when they first meet engage in some form of one-upmanship (my words; I didn't like Mr. Haden's description). This is the "alpha male" conversation. *(Stew's Note: A great example is the lunch conversation between two Type-A personalities when they try and top each other with who they know.)*

Don't try to win the "getting to know someone" competition. Try to lose. Be complimentary. Be impressed. Admit a failing or a weakness.

Don't be afraid to show a little vulnerability. You'll be seen as sincere and genuine.

Be the real you. People will like the real you.

ASK FOR NOTHING.

You know the moment. You're having a great conversation; you're finding things in common . . . and then bam! Someone plays the networking card and puts the hard sell on you.

Everything about your interaction changes at that point. It does with me.

Put away the hard-charging, goal-oriented, always-on kind of persona. If you have to ask for something, find a way first to help the other person and then ask.

Remarkably likable people focus on what they can do for you and not what they can do for themselves. *(Stew's Note: Be a Giver, not a Taker.)*

RECOGNIZE THAT LONG-TERM RELATIONSHIPS ARE BASED ON COOPERATION.

Here are some things to think about when you interact with your referral partners. Please remember that it works both ways:

DEPENDABILITY

- My referral partners are punctual: they return calls and arrive for meetings on time.

- Correspondence and other information owed me arrive on time.

- My referral partners inform me of issues as soon as they arise.

- I can depend on my referral partners to work with me to create win-win solutions.

RESPONSIVENESS

- My referral partners understand my needs.

- My referral partners are sincerely interested in helping me meet my needs.

- When agreements are made, they are kept. We hold each other accountable.

- If challenges arise that make our agreements undoable, we make good, new agreements.

- Do I look forward to working with my referral partners?

CONFLICT RESOLUTION

- I openly communicate issues to my referral partners.

- We view issues as challenges to be resolved rather than things to bring about blame or not deal with.

- I have a well-defined "Issue Resolution" process that I can use with my referral partners.

- My referral partners and I work responsibly to a full resolution when an issue is identified.

- My referral partners and I can discuss lessons learned and make appropriate changes to avoid future challenges.

"CLOSE" GENUINELY.

"Nice to meet you," you say, nodding once as you part. That's the standard move, one that is instantly forgettable. Instead, follow these steps:

- Shake hands again.

- Use your free hand to gently touch the other person's forearm or shoulder.

- Say, "I am really glad I met you," or

- Say, "You know, I really enjoyed talking with you."

- SMILE: Not that insincere salesperson smile that goes with, "Have a nice day!" but a genuine, appreciative smile (and shake your head at the same time).

Making a great first impression is important, but so is making a great last impression.

ACCEPT THE FACT THAT IT ISN'T EASY.

All of this sounds simple, right? For some of us, it is. But it's not easy, especially if you're shy or you haven't practiced. The standard power pose, "Hello, how are you, good to meet you, good seeing you," shuffle feels a lot safer to most of us.

But that won't make people like you or want to do business with you.

So let's accept it's a hard process. Accept that being a little more deferential, a little more genuine, a little more complimentary, and a little more vulnerable means putting yourself out there. Accept that at first it will feel risky.

But don't worry: When you help people feel a little better about themselves—which is reason enough—they'll like you for it.

(Please note that I have quoted directly from Jeff Haden's article as well as paraphrased certain items.)

Highlights

- Social Capital = Better Teamwork = Access to Opportunity

- Social Competence = Increased Chance for Success = Greater Financial Success

- Benefits of social capital: information, influence, collective action, bonding, and bridging.

- Social capital motivations: feeling validation, seeking to belong, and recognizing sympathy for others.

- The three dimensions of social capital: structural, relational, and cognitive.

- You have social capital resources that combined with specific action steps will increase your potential for networking success.

- Lose the power ego stance and make it about them, not you.

- Everyone is better than you at something. Let others be better than you.

- Be a Social Jiu-Jitsu master. Let others talk.

- Cooperation is a very powerful tool.

- Seven -
Networking Strategies

"Approach every networking opportunity with a specific objective. Good results will come from good planning."

                               Margie Bingham
                               Global Recruiters Midtown Nashville
                               Nashville, TN

NETWORKING IS A JOURNEY.

The *JOURNEY* is a *process*.

Step One: "GET THE MINDSET OF NETWORKING"®

- You *MUST* come to the realization that networking has to become an integral part of your personal marketing plan. In today's New World, YOU CAN'T AFFORD *NOT* TO NETWORK ON A FORMAL AND DISCIPLINED BASIS.

- You *MUST* make networking part of your daily business routine.

- You *MUST* get comfortable with networking or hire someone who is. Remember, the Old World isn't coming back. You must be looking forward through the front windshield at the upcoming curve in the road rather than looking back in the rearview mirror at where you've been and hoping the Old World will come back.

- You *MUST* teach yourself to successfully network if networking isn't in your blood. I taught myself, and you can do it too.

- You *MUST* get over any personal obstacles with respect to getting out and meeting people. In other words, if you're an introvert or feel the least bit inhibited, *GET OVER IT*. Force yourself to do it, or hire someone who can do it (and then buy him or her this book).

- You *MUST* approach networking as being a *GIVER* and not a *TAKER*.

- You *MUST* make the commitment to yourself that you will follow the steps necessary to give you the best chance of success and return on your networking investment. This includes a commitment to following networking protocol.

WHAT IS YOUR NETWORKING AND BUSINESS DEVELOPMENT EMOTIONAL STATE RIGHT NOW?

- You *MUST* understand which of the following you are:

WALLFLOWER: You are afraid of networking, are uncomfortable with networking, and break out into a cold sweat when put in a formal networking environment. You'd rather push paper than pick up the phone.

MINIMALIST: You understand the need, but you don't have the time: you're overextended, and you're typically a Taker and not a Giver. Many people see themselves as networkers, but in reality, they are minimalists. They go to networking functions and perhaps join a networking organization but don't do what is necessary to be successful. They will drop out of the networking organization, all the while saying it is the networking organization's fault and not theirs.

NETWORKER: You're engaged, proactive, can effectively verbalize your business to others as well as effectively verbalize how someone can introduce you into an opportunity. You make networking a part of your daily routine. You'd rather be on the phone than push paper.

CONNECTOR: You are always thinking of others and actively connecting people because you understand others' businesses so as to make meaningful introductions.

"Smart people know that the real marketing opportunity lies in how to leverage networking to achieve their goals. It's your focus on the strategy and its successful execution that is important, not the focus on the endgame."

Joel Widmer
Fluxe Digital Marketing
Nashville, TN

Step Two: DEVELOP YOUR STRATEGY.

- First and foremost, *HAVE A GAME PLAN*.

- This is worth repeating: *HAVE A GAME PLAN*.

ADVICE

I highly recommend that you create a personal marketing plan for yourself. It should include the many strategies to pursue as part of your overall marketing game plan. Developing a networking strategy game plan would be a subset of the overall master plan. Why do I think this is important? Because it becomes your road map. It is also something that can help you develop quantitative goals and timelines for personal accountability.

- Develop a **SMART** game plan.

    Specific
    Have you built your game plan with quantitative and qualitative goals?

    Measurable
    Can you easily measure each of the goals in your game plan?

    Achievable
    Have you set realistic and pragmatic goals?

    Resonate
    Does your game plan strike a chord? Is it consistent with your overall goals?

    Time-bound
    Have you built into your game plan an end date for each goal?

- Know what you want to use the tool (your game plan) for. Many strategies involved with putting a game plan together have been covered in the first two chapters. *Your game plan or road map is nothing more than a TOOL.*

STORY

Why do most people who have a profile on LinkedIn never use it as part of their marketing game plan? I'll tell you why. They don't know how to use it and are afraid of it. *LinkedIn is a TOOL.* No more. No less. Most of the seminars given today on LinkedIn teach people how to push buttons or, in other words, how to create a personal profile and that's about it. *PEOPLE ARE NOT TAUGHT HOW TO USE LINKEDIN TO DEVELOP BUSINESS*. It's a tool for developing **BUSINESS THROUGH NETWORKING**.

ADVICE

Networking is nothing more than a TOOL. It is a strategy unto itself. It should be one component of your personal marketing plan. To use this tool effectively, you must understand how you want to use it (i.e., these will be the tactics you will use). You must accept that your primary investment in this tool will be *TIME*.

DON'T UNDERESTIMATE THE POWER OF LAYING A SOLID FOUNDATION, AND REALIZE THAT IT WILL TAKE TIME TO ACHIEVE THE RESULTS THAT YOU EXPECT.

- Determine which networking organization best fits your business model, your expectations, and your personality (see chapter 3). Does the organization have people who are in your target market or do business in your target market?

- Find a networking mentor. Even the best businesspeople have business coaches. Why shouldn't you find the best networking coach or mentor? Meet with your mentor on a regular basis to discuss your successes and areas where you feel you need help. The best business coach will set objectives and hold you accountable.

ADVICE

Find a mentor partner within the networking organization that you ultimately join. The person you want is a proven networker and belongs to the elite status of a *CONNECTOR*.

- Approach the networking process as though you are building business partnerships.

- Use the litmus test of **TRUST** in developing your key networking partnerships. The question you must ask is, "Can I trust this person?"

- Set realistic goals for the first year of your involvement in a networking organization. Break down your goals (and ultimate success) into smaller chunks. For example, determine a minimum goal for each networking meeting.

Step Three: EXECUTE YOUR GAME PLAN.

You can have the best mindset and the best game plan, but if *YOU DON'T EXECUTE* the game plan on a consistent basis, you will fail.

Remember that building *TRUST* with others takes time.

I am terrible at cold calling. I loved doing it and I was very good at getting

STORY

my proverbial foot in the door, but I could never develop an adequate follow-up process: out of sight, out of mind. You won't be successful in cold calling or any marketing strategy without a process for follow-up. Networking was a process that I developed for myself, and it became part of my daily routine.

PRAGMATIC ASSESSMENTS = MAXIMUM RESULTS

Step Four: MAINTAIN AN INFORMAL SCORING SYSTEM.

Many networking organizations use this strategy to hold their members accountable. I don't believe in quota systems (i.e., the quantitative scoring systems). However, I do believe in keeping score on an informal basis. There are two methods that I believe should be used in a culture that promotes a formal and disciplined approach to networking.

- When I give a referral to someone, I expect him or her to reciprocate, perhaps not immediately but at some point in the future.

STORY

Remember the story I told in an earlier chapter about one of my members giving a local attorney nine referrals in one year? The attorney booked all nine referrals, and my member never got anything in return. If after talking to the attorney I felt that he didn't get it, I would likely not send him any further referrals. There are plenty of good attorneys with whom I can establish a relationship, and they will reciprocate.

- I use a multitiered approach to ranking the people I meet. You've likely seen this in other marketing books as a pyramid, an inverted triangle, or circles within circles. I just keep it simple. I call this *THE NETWORKING MATRIX*.

LEVEL C

This is your *NETWORKING UNIVERSE*. This is everyone you meet.

LEVEL B

These are the ones who think of you and refer at least one piece of business or several introductions consistently each year.

LEVEL A

These are the handful of people who consistently refer business to you. You are their "go to" person. You're lucky to have 3 or 4 of these. They tend to be become your personal friends.

This approach or process is ever changing. It is not a static process. In other words, you are moving people up and down between the levels, depending on their activity with you. Remember that I said you have to annually reevaluate the networking and professional organizations you're in? Well, you have to do that with the folks you refer business to.

This all sounds mercenary, doesn't it? Well, to a certain extent it is. It's all part of the culture that promotes the formal and disciplined approach to networking.

DON'T FORGET TO RECIPROCATE on those B and A relationships.

STORY

I ran a commercial banking group in Los Angeles, and I hired a long-time banker who was one of the most accomplished networkers I had ever seen. Eighteen months later we had to let this banker go. Why? He was amazing at building his Level C or the "universe" as I like to call it. His problem was that he couldn't convert Level C people into Level B referral sources. The result was no business.

ADVICE

Train yourself to look at people as potential referral sources, and classify them into the three networking levels. In that compartment in your brain labeled "Networking," have a picture of the levels and always keep moving people between them. Set a goal of having five referral sources in the Level A category.

Step Five: DEVELOP A LONG-TERM STRATEGY.

TEACH YOURSELF TO GO BEYOND NETWORKING AND BECOME A CONNECTOR.

As you will see in the last chapter, your long-term strategy is to become a **CONNECTOR**.

Once you become a connector, you really have taken your skill set to the next level and enhanced your networking skills. Not everyone is at the *CONNECTOR STATUS*. If you can reach that level, you will further differentiate yourself from the competition.

Highlights

- Networking is a journey. The journey is a process.

- Put yourself into the right mindset. You must realize that networking has to become part of your daily routine.

- Determine your current activity level: wallflower, minimalist, networker, or connector.

- Develop your strategy through your game plan. Your plan must be specific, measurable, achievable, resonate, and time-bound. It is your road map to success.

- Find someone who can be your networking mentor. Meet with him or her on a regular basis.

- Build trust through business partnerships.

- Execute on your game plan. The alternative is failure.

- You should maintain an informal scoring system if you are to follow a formal and disciplined networking agenda.

- Develop your own Networking Matrix. Move your referral partners up or down on the matrix, depending on their level of activity with you. Don't forget to reciprocate.

- Develop a long-term strategy that takes you to the next level: CONNECTOR status.

- Eight -

Networking Tactics

"Have you ever been in a meeting and the other person said they were going to do something yet did not take notes? Don't be that 'other' person; this seems simple, but bring a pen and take notes; you'll record your follow-ups and you'll be able to remind them later of their commitments to you."

Steve Minucci
The Tenney Group
Nashville, TN

Decide up front to set aside time each day to network.

It's critical that you build this into your daily routine. The various components that you can use are as follows:

1. **Telephone:** Check in with clients, prospects, or referral partners.

2. **Coffee, lunch, or breakfast:** Do not eat alone. Try to schedule two per day; you'll typically be scheduling two weeks out.

3. **Networking Meetings:** Go to formal group meetings or one-on-one meetings.

4. **E-mail:** Send out informational messages to your audience. I use e-mail to send copies of pertinent articles to folks I think might be interested in reading them, either business related or something that I know is of interest (e.g., a hobby).

5. **LinkedIn:** Spend at least fifteen minutes a day on LinkedIn once you know HOW you want to use this tool.

6. **Entertainment Events**: Identify clients, prospects, or referral partners who have children. Then suggest an event centered on the children (e.g., circus, ice-skating show, musical theater, etc.). It means more to the parents than a hockey game (unless their kids are into hockey).

STORY

I was reading an interview given to the *Wall Street Journal* by Anna Wintour, editor of *Vogue* magazine. She abruptly ended the interview by telling the interviewer that it was time for her to begin her daily hour of networking (via the phone). You would think that a person in her position would not need to formally network. Ms. Wintour recognizes the power of networking and has set aside a block of time each day to do it. Now that's what I call a *formal and disciplined* approach to networking. I was impressed.

Remember the important thing in accomplishing something: YOU MUST SHOW UP.

Sounds simple, huh? It's true. Showing up is a *TACTIC*. You must make the commitment to show up to the networking events that you've paid for. What do they say, "Out of sight, out of mind"?

When you join a networking organization (or any other formal type of group), I suspect that it meets on a particular day of the week or month. Well, put it on your calendar as a recurring event for the entire year. Schedule your clients or other appointments around that day and time. Yes, I know that sometimes a client calls up and needs to see you at the time that conflicts with your networking meeting. If it's not the deal of the century, try to get the client to meet a couple of hours later. In more than thirty years of banking, I never ran into a situation where a two-hour difference meant life or death to a client. *IT'S PART OF BEING COMMITTED TO THE NETWORKING PROCESS.*

The number one reason I suspect that people drop their memberships in health clubs is that they stop going. I experience the same dynamics in the networking organization.

If you can't make your usually scheduled group meeting, visit another group. Most good networking organizations will allow you to visit other groups or chapters. This is a value-added service that is for the benefit of members.

Even if you are a regular attendee for your group or chapter meeting, you may want to commit to visiting at least one other group or chapter meeting that month. Not only are you meeting others that you typically wouldn't get to meet, but also you can identify one or two people to follow up for one-on-one meetings.

When you attend your regular meetings, come prepared with a list of people and companies that you would like introductions to. You do have your "Top 25" prospect list, don't you? Use it in your networking efforts.

ADVICE

In Los Angeles, the six degrees of separation were really a maximum of four. I could get to the California governor with four calls (and I did). In Nashville, it really is one degree and, at the most, two. So the odds are very high that someone in the group or chapter will know the person in a particular company you need an introduction to.

Be engaged and proactive in the process.

If you aren't, I guarantee that your expectations won't be met. Although there never are any guarantees, your chances for success will be very high if you are engaged and proactive. Your success will be exponential to your level of involvement.

STORY

In Nashville, people do not talk in terms of absolute dollars. So you won't hear someone talk about how much money he made as a result of a referral. So right after midyear, I asked five of my members how much money they made in the first six months as a result of a direct referral from other Business Forum members. I picked the five members because they were engaged and proactive in our process. When I added it up, it totaled $810,000, and that represented only five members and five deals.

Don't ever eat alone.

Keith Ferrazzi wrote the book *Never Eat Alone*. The book jacket is a bright orange, a *BRILLIANT MOVE BY MR. FERRAZZI*. Experts tell me that three things sell a book: title, cover, and pictures. There's only one problem in my opinion. Mr. Ferrazzi's title tells you the whole story, so why buy the book?

There's more to it obviously than just the title. He's right, though. In sales, why would you ever want to eat alone when you could have the opportunity to break bread with a client, a prospect, or a referral source?

ADVICE

On a conventional five-day workweek, you have ten opportunities to take someone out for a meal (breakfast and lunch times five). I recognized that setting a goal of ten meals per week was somewhat unrealistic. So my personal goal was eight times a week I would take a client, a prospect, or a referral source out for a meal. Heck, you've got a boss who expects you to make a certain minimum number of calls each month, don't you? In my case, I knocked out one-third of the required monthly calls with this philosophy. Besides you might as well have a good meal doing it, even though you'll always have to fight the boss on the expense account. Good bosses recognize that it takes a dollar to make a hundred.

Determine the sales cycle category for your product or service.

This analysis will determine whether you think in terms of short-term, intermediate, or long-term expectations. Networking organizations that specialize in leads are typically more short-term oriented (i.e., transactional based) than the organizations that emphasize the culture of building long-term relationships.

TRANSACTIONAL: This is a one-time transaction for the most part. The sales cycle is typically shorter so there's capacity for a greater number of transactions. Usually, it's easy to describe what you do or sell. It makes sense to join multiple networking organizations.

TRANSACTIONAL/RELATIONSHIP: This is the typical arrangement for most of us. We like to think that it is weighted toward the relationship end, and it likely is. If you are starting off your career, perhaps a leads-type organization is best. If you are in the middle or later part of your career, a senior-level networking organization might be best. You really need to look at your current client base and match it appropriately.

PURE RELATIONSHIP: I think the best example would be a wealth advisor. The sales cycle can be very long and is typically driven by referral or word of mouth. You are planting the seeds for future referrals. Your expectations for business referrals should not be as high as those of the transactional person. You should be very choosy about a networking organization. A senior-level organization is likely the best candidate for you.

This will help you determine *how many* as well as the *type* of networking organizations to join. You need to have a good handle on this because it will help you when setting your expectations for the number of referrals.

Identify the business verticals that encompass the immediate circle around you and your business.

To me this is probably one of the most important tactics to successful networking. Look around at the people you do business with. Who tends to touch the potential clients you'd like to have? Identify the verticals but not the people. These are the business verticals that will be in the first circle around you (i.e., immediate synergy). Once you've identified the verticals, now you can start identifying the people who fill those verticals. THEY ARE THE PEOPLE YOU WANT TO BE INTRODUCED TO AND ULTIMATELY DEVELOP INTO REFERRAL PARTNERSHIPS.

EXAMPLE

An executive recruiter whose product and service center on determining the right "fit" between the prospective employee and a particular job description would want to start with the verticals in the Human Resource arena. Identify those particular verticals that touch their product, and focus on those folks.

You will also want to identify the second circle around you. These would be the business verticals that have similar calling patterns and the ability to connect you with the folks in the first circle. An example might be people who design websites. While they wouldn't likely have direct synergy with the person who sells computers, these folks "touch" the end users of websites.

Take the "Rifle" approach versus the "Shotgun" approach.

What I just described above is taking the "Rifle" approach versus the "Shotgun" approach. Don't start inviting people to meet with you just for the sake of getting to meet a lot of people. *You waste your time, their time, and your money.* This is an *EFFICIENCY* tactic.

Be Selective In Who You Want To Meet.

Take a focused approach to determining who might have the most synergy over time with you. If you're a banker in the middle market, you will want to develop friendships with CPAs, corporate attorneys, commercial P&C insurance people, and anyone who is in direct contact with middle-market companies and their owners. The second circle might include the real estate broker who handles corporate relocations.

Why would I as a senior commercial banker reach out and actively pursue the person who is a consultant specializing in language translation? This vertical not only doesn't fit the first circle; it doesn't fit the second circle around what the banker does.

I don't mean to suggest that you disregard people; I'm not saying that at all! When I meet the language consultant, I still want to make a good impression with her. You never know where a referral might come from in the future. What I'm telling you is that when you craft your networking game plan, you must be pragmatic about who you target as a potential networking partner.

Novice networkers too often make the mistake when they join a networking organization of thinking that everyone in the group will be a networking partner. It won't happen for many reasons. Get to know everyone, but be selective in the formal process of identifying long-term referral partners.

STORY Two of my members (in two different industries) figured out that the basic profile of their client/prospect base was very similar. They got together and compared their clients as well as their prospect list. After that, they developed an action plan to work together to refer business to one another.

Reassess your involvement in ALL organizations on an annual basis.

As someone who owns and runs a networking organization, I'd love to have all of you stay with me forever. However, I'm realistic enough to know that you have limited time and money. You must make decisions based on deployment of limited resources of time and money and the return you get on those resources. Everyone has different motivations for joining a networking organization, and I'm not about to try and figure out everyone.

On an annual basis, it is prudent to reassess the organizations of which you are a member. That goes for ALL organizations and not just pure networking ones. Your resources change from year to year. Your expectations will change.

One of our members was promoted, and the job responsibilities changed. He was now targeting large Fortune 500 companies. He recognized that our "sweet spot" was not Fortune 500 companies. So he resigned. I fully understood and would have advised him to do that.

As you go through the process each year, you must be truthful with yourself. In other words, if your reason for resigning from an organization is that your expectations were not met, sit back and ask yourself whether it was the organization's fault or your fault for perhaps not being more involved.

Bring guests to your networking organization.

Most networking organizations want their members to bring guests. The lifeblood of a networking organization (at least for mine it is) will be guests. The organization will grow as these guests become members. This leads to more people sitting around the table, and the existing members will benefit from the new relationships.

One correlation that I have noticed over time is that the members who sponsor guests at our chapter meetings tend to be the members who are engaged and proactive in our process. They are also the members who make the most money through the referral and introduction process.

But let's look at this from a tactical and pragmatic perspective. My members are always asking me about which persons they should bring as guests. I've tried many ways to assist them with this.

I've tried to simplify the decision-making process for them. *START WITH QUALITY*. Look for someone who is a *QUALITY* individual. Next look for someone in a vertical that is Business-to-Business or at least a portion of the business is. Then look at the person and ask whether networking is in his or her DNA.

Why don't you invite people who can help you? Is there someone that you reached out to in the past, but for some reason it got shoved under the rug? Why not invite that person to be your guest? It's a good way to jump-start a potential valuable relationship. Another tactic would be to reach out to someone you wish you knew and invite her or him. You've added value to someone who will remember you.

Attend networking events in addition to your organization's chapter meetings.

I've said it before, "out of sight, out of mind."

People need to see you and talk with you before they will be comfortable with you. Going to your monthly (or weekly) chapter meetings isn't enough. If your networking organization sponsors other events, then you should attend. Every time I initially hesitated going to an event but finally ended up going, I was thankful that I attended. I always met one person who made the event worthwhile. My reaction was always, "Man, am I glad I went."

When you attend networking events you should do the following:

- Sit with different people each month.

- Come early and stay late.

- Don't try to collect everyone's business card.

- Be focused on who you want to meet, and get their business cards.

- Obtain a list of who will be attending the meeting if you can.

- Follow up immediately if you make a promise to someone.

- Make it a goal to identify at least one person you should follow up with after the meeting.

- Put your own Troika group together each month if your networking organization doesn't practice the Troika subgroup process.

- Verbally thank people during the meeting. Make it a goal to thank at least one person at each meeting. A testimonial is a very powerful tool to create, maintain, and deepen relationships with your networking partners. People *EXPECT YOU* to do this after they have gone out of their way to make that referral or introduction. *DON'T YOU EXPECT THAT WHEN THE ROLES ARE REVERSED*?

Learn how to work a room when you don't know anyone.

This title was a facilitated discussion at one of our chapter meetings. It was probably one of the better discussions we've had since it's a common problem for most people, whether they will admit it or not.

Who isn't intimidated when walking into a room where you don't know anyone? If there's one thing you must always remember, it's that . . .

EVERYONE FEELS THE SAME WAY YOU DO.

- When you meet people for the first time, let them do the talking. People like to talk about themselves. If you let them talk, they will think much higher of you than if you do all the talking.

- Be a good LISTENER. Remember H A Beasley's quote in an earlier chapter? H A says, "Listening is a competitive advantage."

- When and how should you put yourself into a group? If there are two people talking together and they are face-to-face, you should not interrupt (it is likely they are in a private conversation). If the two people are standing at an angle, it is appropriate to join them. Wait for them to break their conversation and for one of them to acknowledge you.

- What if you are one of the two people having a private conversation and someone interrupts? It is appropriate for you to say to that person, "I'm sorry, but we are having a private conversation. Would it be all right if I talk with you in a moment?" Make sure that you seek out that person once you have completed your conversation.

- Getting out of a group to get into another group is not hard. All you have to do is excuse yourself.

- When you are in a conversation with someone, don't keep looking away. Don't keep looking for the next person to talk with. *IT'S RUDE.* The other person doesn't think you're interested in him or what he has to say. Maybe it's true, and you don't. But it's better to move on than it is to appear rude.

- If you have to end the conversation for whatever reason, let the other person know that you have some others to meet at this function, but you will look for any meaningful introductions to make to her.

- How hard do you shake a lady's hand? We asked this question of our lady members. The consensus was that two types of handshakes were unacceptable: the "limp fish handshake" and the "bone crusher handshake."

- Don't enter the room and immediately put the appetizer plate in one hand and the drink in the other hand. *HOW IN THE WORLD WILL YOU BE ABLE TO SHAKE ANYONE'S HAND?*

- ALWAYS wear your name badge on the right lapel. Why? Because when someone extends a hand to shake yours, his eyes immediately go to the left and focus on your name.

- How can you remember so many people's names? One trick is to say the person's name at least three times. The first time is when you meet someone: "Hi, Stew, it's good to meet you." The second time would be at some point during the discussion: "You know, Stew, you're absolutely correct." The third and last time is when the conversation is over: "Stew, I can't tell you what a pleasure it's been meeting you."

- Immediately after the function, take the business cards you've collected and separate them into two piles: people to follow up with and all the others. Write on their cards short, meaningful comments about them.

- Within twenty-four hours, follow up with those people you feel warrant a second meeting. If you wait longer than seventy-two hours to follow up with someone, you might as well not make the effort.

- Oh, and by the way, don't show up to a networking event without any business cards. It will leave the opposite message you really want to leave with someone.

ADVICE Tom Black (Tom Black Center for Excellence) says, "Successful people form the habit of doing the things unsuccessful people don't want to do." You are at a competitive advantage by learning how to work a room.

Make sure that the person you meet with understands two things:

- What you do, stated in a very basic way.

- How she or he can recognize an opportunity to introduce you into a potential revenue situation.

If you can't articulate the message you want someone to hear, whose fault is it that you don't get the referrals or introductions you expect?

IT'S YOUR RESPONSIBILITY TO GET YOUR MESSAGE ACROSS TO OTHERS

AND

TO TRAIN PEOPLE ON HOW TO RECOGNIZE REFERRAL OPPORTUNITIES.

Before you end the meeting, you might want to ask a couple of questions to see if the person really understands what you do and how to recognize that special opportunity. You might want to ask, "Can you suggest any improvements on getting my message across about what I do?"

You should always give your potential referral partners one question they should know to ask their clients in order to recognize the opportunity to introduce you. An example might be someone who designs websites. He might say to me, "One way to recognize an opportunity is to ask your clients, 'Has your website administrator introduced search engine optimization?'"

Leave copies of your "One-Sheet" (refer to the Appendix for an example) with people. Let them know that you will follow up with an electronic version of the "One-Sheet." More and more people are creating electronic files to store such information for future reference.

Ask the group leader if it is okay to bring your "One-Sheet" to the regular networking meetings and hand them out. I would never turn down that request from members or guests. That's what we're all about.

Make referral commitments to others.

This tactic should be used on networking partners that you are already comfortable with or with a potential networking partner that you feel somehow has not connected with you.

STORY

A person in one of my Los Angeles networking groups represented the insurance P&C vertical. He and I discovered that we actually shared some clients. Somehow he and I never connected on a formal basis. So one day I invited him to lunch and explained that I would like to commit to a monthly lunch with him and that I would guarantee to have one referral for him at each lunch. I have to admit that it lasted only four lunches. The scorecard read: Referrals from Stew - FOUR; Referrals back to Stew from P&C guy - ZERO. I moved on, but it doesn't mean it can't work.

ADVICE

Assuming you feel comfortable enough with someone to do this, you might want to consider setting up some sort of quid pro quo system. In other words, you give me an introduction or referral, and I commit to you that I will reciprocate. This type of relationship takes networking to a higher level. It becomes an accountability issue. It also puts the relationship on the highest level of networking, and typically, these types of referral partners become social friends.

Reach out to other members of your networking organization.

Make it part of your monthly routine to reach out to at least two or three other members of your networking or professional organization. As a member, you should have access to the contact information for ALL members.

At each monthly chapter meeting of the Southeast Business Forums, we assign everyone who attends (member and guest) to a Troika. This is where we put three people together to meet over a cup of coffee. I tell everyone that if they hear someone's introduction and they feel the need to meet this person but are not assigned to that individual's Troika, then reach out to him outside our formal process. Our real networkers and connectors do this routinely.

Use Social Media as a tool in your networking efforts.

I'll be the first to admit that I am no expert in social media. I've been pulled into it kicking and screaming. Building a business called the Southeast Business Forums has forced me to become much more technologically savvy than I ever was before (my generation got caught between the slide rule and the personal computer). Writing this book and self-publishing have forced me to embrace social media as a means of marketing to a select audience. Frankly, it's been fun.

I highly recommend that you build and use social media to complement your networking tactics. Unfortunately, I do not feel comfortable enough in my knowledge to give you specific tactics in this regard. There are people and organizations that can build these platforms for you. As you network, try to meet these types of folks. I have, and it has been enlightening.

The one social media component that I do know something about is LinkedIn. I consider LinkedIn to be the biggest breakthrough in mass networking that we've ever seen. It is a tremendously powerful tool. Executive recruiters are masters of this tool. I suggest you make friends with an executive recruiter and learn how to use LinkedIn as a tool in your networking efforts.

When we were building the dedicated LinkedIn site for the Southeast Business Forums, we learned a couple of things. First, 99% of the business population has some sort of a profile on LinkedIn. Of that population, less than 10% actually use LinkedIn as a tool to assist in building their business.

We found that there were two primary reasons why people did not actively use LinkedIn:

- First, they were *NEVER TAUGHT HOW* to use LinkedIn. The seminars taught them how to set up a profile and "push buttons" but never taught them the tactics and strategies for using the tool.

- Second, they are afraid to use LinkedIn because of the perceived "black hole of time" that would engulf them. This goes back to the first issue. If you know exactly how you want to use this tool we call LinkedIn, you will be very efficient with your time.

STORY One of our members is very adept at using LinkedIn. A lot of his business is derived from using LinkedIn and in particular the LinkedIn groups. He uses LinkedIn every day and is on it no more than fifteen to twenty minutes each day. He knows exactly how to use LinkedIn and what he wants to get out of it. No "black hole of time" for him.

Eight: Networking Tactics

ADVICE

If you aren't using LinkedIn every day in your prospecting and networking efforts, you are missing opportunities. Find a seminar that will teach you the tactics and strategies of using LinkedIn. If you can't find a seminar, hire a consultant to teach you. Determine HOW you want to use the tool, and then START to use it. It is worth it.

Create an effective thirty-second elevator speech.

You have about one minute to make either a favorable or an unfavorable impression on someone you meet for the first time on an individual basis or in a group setting. Your brand is both professional and personal. It is also verbal and visual.

You set the visual brand within the first several seconds: it is your appearance. You get a little bit longer to set the verbal brand, but it, too, is limited. In today's world, people's attention spans are not what they used to be. You get about thirty to forty-five seconds to get your point across.

"ENTHUSIASM SELLS, SO USE IT IN YOUR ELEVATOR SPEECH."

> **Tom Black**
> Tom Black Center for Excellence

ADVICE

Leave your *EGO* at the door. The person you're talking to must know how *YOU* will fit into *HIS* world. **TELL HIM**.

The first thing you want to do is create that elevator speech. Please visit the Appendix of this book, and I will walk you through that process.

Highlights

- Make the commitment to set aside time each day to network.

- Show up to your events.

- Be engaged and proactive in the networking process if you want to have a chance of being successful.

- Never eat alone.

- Identify business verticals that fit into the first circle or orbit around your business. The folks who fit into those verticals are the ones you will have the most synergy with. This will help you take the "rifle" approach to networking.

- Perform an annual assessment of all the organizations to which you belong. Your resources—time and money—are limited.

- Bring guests to your networking organization's meetings.

- Remember the problem of being out of sight, out of mind. Attend all the events held by your networking organization.

- Never overlook that listening is a competitive advantage.

- Always make sure the person you meet with walks away UNDERSTANDING TWO THINGS: first, what you do, and second, how SHE can recognize an opportunity to introduce you into a potential revenue situation. Provide one question she should remember to ask a client to recognize that opportunity.

- Create an effective thirty-second elevator speech that can be adapted for different situations.

- Nine -

Troika Best Practices

"I receive a lot of referrals through the Southeast Business Forums, and the overwhelming majority of them come immediately following a Troika. A person who does not participate in an assigned Troika is probably leaving a lot of money on the table and not getting the most out of their networking."

Bill Watson
Advanced Business Group
Nashville, TN

DEFINITION

TROIKA is defined by *Merriam-Webster Dictionary*: "a group of three." Its origins are in the Russian language troika, from *troe*, three.

Numerous networking groups, including Southeast Business Forums, use the term *Troika* to denote assigned groups of three to get together for the purpose of networking.

First of all, this book is intended to present a generic approach to networking rather than any individual networking organization's specific approach or process.

It is inevitable, however, that references to my networking organization will creep into our discussion. It's a process that works for many people, and I'd be remiss by not including certain parts of the process.

I did not invent the Troika. I learned about and experienced the Troika while being a member in several high-level networking organizations in Los Angeles. So when I developed the networking business model called "The Southeast Business Forums," I knew that I had to incorporate the Troika into our organization. *Why?*

Because The Troika Is The Beginning Of The Process Known As "The Mindset Of Networking®."

This is where three members/guests get together for a cup of coffee, breakfast, or lunch to begin to build individual relationships. It is a time for each of them to discuss their respective businesses in greater detail, describe how they get their new business, and find out how they can assist each other in making referrals and introductions in the future.

Yes, the Troika process is an integral and differentiating segment of the Southeast Business Forums culture. The reason for including it as an individual chapter in this book is that . . .

THE PRINCIPLES (OR "BEST PRACTICES") OF A TROIKA HOLD TRUE FOR ANY EFFECTIVE NETWORKING PROCESS, WHETHER IT'S IN A CROWD, ONE-ON-ONE, OR SOMEWHERE IN BETWEEN.

The *TROIKA BEST PRACTICES* are guidelines you can follow and adapt to virtually any networking situation. Again, this isn't that hard. It's just plain old good common sense (at least to me it is).

ADVICE — Unless there is a death in the family or an illness, *SHOW UP* to your Troika. If you can't make it, let your Troika partners know in advance.

Remember chapter 4, "Networking Protocol"? That was the discussion about your networking reputation and credibility. Well, I'm here to tell you that if you don't follow some of these "Troika Best Practices," your reputation will suffer. I've seen it firsthand.

INITIATE A TROIKA (or any meeting for that matter).

- Members are required to initiate the Troika meeting. A guest should never be put in the position of feeling the need to initiate the Troika.

ADVICE — This is something that I recommend in all instances, not just Troikas. If you have made a promise to do something for someone, you are part of something to be scheduled (e.g., Troika), or a commitment has been made, write it down at the meeting, and THEN FOLLOW THROUGH AS SOON AS YOU GET BACK TO THE OFFICE! Lack of follow-up can hurt your reputation. This goes without saying once you get your Troika assignment.

ADVICE Always be the first to initiate a meeting. Whoever responds first has the opportunity to control the process of where and when.

- When suggesting a day, time, and venue, let your Troika partners know where your office is. This way, it is easier to suggest a venue that is central to each of you.

- Choose a venue that is quiet (or relatively so), has enough room to meet, and offers adequate parking. Some folks don't have a problem meeting at the office of one of the Troika partners. Personally, I believe the meeting venue should be a neutral location.

- Don't give up just because the three of you can't agree the first, second, or even third time. Just acknowledge that coordinating three very busy schedules can be difficult.

- Some people like to use Outlook calendar for the invitation so that it shows up on everyone's calendar.

- How long should you allow for a Troika? I think the best allotment is one hour. If everyone stays on task, this amount of time should accomplish the goals set out by the Troika members.

- In our organization, sponsoring members should set the expectations for their guests. This includes their participation in the Troika.

COME PREPARED.

In other words, do your homework. Not only will this give you an advantage, but your Troika partners will benefit from it as you begin the discussion at a higher level.

- Research your Troika partners, using websites, LinkedIn profiles, and so on.

- Have three to five names of people or companies for which you need introductions.

- Make sure you can articulate your business in a professional and succinct manner.

- Make sure you have a brief case study that illustrates (simply) what you do and how you fix problems. Come with three real problems that you can solve or have solved.

- Have a goal in mind for your Troika partners. If there are people in the meeting you are comfortable with, try to have at least one introduction (or referral) for them.

- Hand out marketing collateral material if you wish.

- Focus on the reality that the Troika is a BUSINESS MEETING.

FOLLOW TROIKA ETIQUETTE.

One very simple idea: *IT'S NOT ABOUT ME.*

- *Do Not* MONOPOLIZE the conversation. You need to be an active listener.

- Give everyone an equal chance to speak.

- *Be* GENUINE. *Be* HONEST.

- This is *NOT* the time to be selling. YOU MUST EARN the right to "ASK."

- Let the guest go first in introducing herself and her business, but ask her first to make sure she is comfortable doing this.

- This is the time to make sure that *YOU WILL BE REMEMBERED.*

- *Be prepared* to step in and "FACILITATE" the Troika discussion if it's not going anywhere or is headed down an inappropriate path. In other words, someone needs to act as the orchestra leader in guiding the Troika discussion. If one person monopolizes the discussion, someone will need to step in and redirect. We typically find that the facilitator happens organically.

- For fairness' sake, not everyone we've talked to believes there should be a formal facilitator. I tend to facilitate from the start only because that's my nature and personality.

- Make sure that you have the mobile phone numbers (and possibly e-mail addresses) of the other Troika partners. This way you can contact them if something comes up at the last minute and you are detained or can't make it.

- If you can't make an introduction (willingly or not), it's okay to say "NO" to the request.

STORY

My wife has worked for a large but privately held company for thirty-six years. It is a company that is well-known, and EVERYONE wants to do business with it. Over the years, I have been spectacularly UNSUCCESSFUL in getting my business clients, friends, and networking acquaintances into the company with an introduction. I learned that I had to say "NO" whenever someone asked me if I could get him an audience with the company.

- Don't say yes and then *NOT* follow through.

- *Leave out* any discussions on POLITICS and RELIGION. Business networking is just that: BUSINESS.

- *Go DUTCH TREAT:* it is best if EVERYONE PAYS FOR HIMSELF or HERSELF.

- Try to balance the discussion between business and personal. You must get a sense for which direction the discussion is going and the comfort level of your partners.

REMEMBER THAT A TROIKA IS A BUSINESS MEETING.

This is essentially similar to the etiquette portion. However, I think we need to frame it within the context of the business meeting:

- Dress appropriately for a business meeting. This doesn't mean a three-piece suit is necessary. But it also doesn't mean showing up in torn jeans and a tee shirt.

- Remain sensitive to others' feelings. This is a time to be politically correct. Save the political, religious, or any other controversial topics for another day with people you know well.

- Discuss a recent legal decision or law that affects businesspeople without making it a political fight. Keep to the facts and not the spin.

- Do not swear in the presence of others. You may lose opportunities.

- Remember that *NOT ALL* business meetings go well. *YOU WILL* experience Troikas when you will think, *Gosh, that was a waste of my time*. Get over it and move on.

- Enjoy the experience when a Troika knocks your socks off. Most referrals or introductions come as a result of the Troika, at the Troika, or immediately after the Troika.

- Choose this best tactic in a Troika (or any other similar type of networking engagement): Ask the other members or guests, "How can I help you?" This is a VERY POWERFUL question.

USE A TROIKA MEETING TO YOUR ADVANTAGE.

This is how to use a Troika meeting as a strategic tool.

YOUR FIRST AND ONLY GOAL IN THE TROIKA IS TO EDUCATE YOUR TROIKA PARTNERS ON HOW TO RECOGNIZE AN OPPORTUNITY TO INTRODUCE YOU.

- Use the Troika to determine who is NOT a good fit for you as a networking partner. We typically concentrate on who will be a good networking partner. We don't spend enough time on analyzing who would NOT be an appropriate partner.

- **COACH** your fellow networking partners on how to present you or identify an opportunity to introduce you.

- **CONNECT** on a PERSONAL LEVEL if you can. Ask them what was the path that led them to where they are today.

- Identify members or guests who are in your "first" circle, and then request a specific Troika partner to be assigned to your Troika.

- Use the Troika to establish and identify common ground.

- Listen carefully to what problems your Troika partners can fix. Perhaps your clients are experiencing these problems, and this will represent an opportunity for you to make an introduction. You will look good to your clients by helping them solve a problem that lies outside your area of expertise.

- Understand that this is part of the process of determining the character of others.

- Go beyond your elevator speech. Give your Troika partners something that will make them want to schedule a one-on-one meeting with you for the purpose of digging even deeper.

- Remember that the Troika experience can be what you and the other Troika partners want it to be (make sure everyone wants to head down that path together).

A member come up to me once and remarked that he had just had the most wonderful Troika experience. He was jazzed about the level of business discussion. The following week, another member approached me and remarked that he had just had the most wonderful Troika experience. Why? The entire discussion centered on the families and kids of each Troika participant. Go figure.

- Educate others on how they can assist you. This is a very important concept. When do you get the opportunity to have others sit in front of you, and THEY MUST LISTEN to what you have to say?

- DO NOT leave the Troika meeting without making sure you KNOW that your Troika partners really know (a) what you do and (b) how to recognize an opportunity for an introduction.

- Recognize that how people show up at a Troika is an indication of how they might manage their business. In other words, are they engaged in the conversation, do they truly act interested in the other members of the conversation, how well are they dressed, and did they come prepared? Doesn't it send a bad signal when someone says, "Gotcha" after every sentence you say and then at the end of the meeting asks a question that really indicates he didn't get it?

ADVICE

Anytime that I had a meeting with a prospect, I expected to walk away with something. Depending on the situation, I knew beforehand what I wanted to get out of the meeting. It's no different with a Troika or any meeting with a potential referral partner. I suggest that you have THREE goals at Troika or networking meetings. First, you need to assimilate the others and determine if these are potential referral partners. Second, you must make sure they understand in very simple terms what you do. Third, leave them with a question that can be used to identify potential opportunities for an introduction.

- Identify and discuss what an ideal client looks like for you.

- Always have one example that you can give people that paints the picture of what you do, how you do it, and how it fixed a problem.

How many times have you gone to a large networking function and walked away knowing that you've just developed a deep and long-lasting relationship with the people you met at the function? I've never experienced that. REMEMBER:

People Do Business With People They Like.

WHAT IF I THINK ONE OF THE TROIKA PARTNERS IS IRRELEVANT?

Why did I place this under its own heading? Because when I hear a member complain about not understanding why the guest in the Troika was invited to one of our networking chapter meetings, let alone the Troika, I just scratch my head.

What do you consider makes a successful day for you from a professional standpoint? For me, one aspect of a successful day is getting to meet someone new. I've been to meetings with folks that I'm not sure I'll ever see again, interact professionally with, or know what type of impression I've made on them.

It never ceases to amaze me when sometimes these "irrelevant" guests come back in the future with introductions. If you want to be successful in your networking efforts, you must see the BIG PICTURE.

STORY

One of our members invited someone to be our guest at a chapter meeting. Our guest was not from Nashville but was in the process of relocating. Once he got to Nashville, our guest (who did not have a job at the time) started introducing others to me, and we actually obtained several new members as a result. Over time, I would run into others who knew this individual and had similar results. Just an example of never knowing when or where that next referral will come from.

THE TROIKA IS PART OF THE PROCESS CALLED "THE MINDSET OF NETWORKING®."

GENERAL NETWORKING EVENT

TROIKA

ONE-ON-ONE
(This can be step 2 if the Troika is not involved.)

Seems like a no-brainer, huh? You're thinking, *I paid for this book, and this is the simplistic stuff Stew is showing me? What an idiot I am!*

No, you're not. You wouldn't believe how many people either don't grasp this simple concept or won't make the investment in time to follow the steps needed to grow their business (assuming they want to grow it, but that's for another day and another discussion).

Do you really feel that you are in *CONTROL* of everything around you? This process is something that is within your control.

You Can Control This Process If You Put Your Mind To It.

Networking is like having an *ANNUITY*. If you make the right investments, those relationships will continue to pay off throughout your career.

Highlights

- A Troika is a group of three people who come together for the purpose of getting to know one another, their respective businesses, and what makes a good referral and determining whether there is the potential for being a future referral partner.

- A Troika event is a networking event. So prepare and act accordingly.

- Be the first to initiate the meeting: date, time, and venue.

- Troika etiquette: IT'S NOT ABOUT YOU.

- The most important question you can ask, "How can I help you?"

- Your TWO most important goals in a Troika: first, make sure that each person knows what you do, stated in simple terms, and second, make sure when others leave the meeting, they know how to recognize an opportunity to introduce you.

- Coach your referral partners on how to introduce you.

- Networking is a process you can control on the macro and the micro levels. The Troika meeting is the first step in managing the process.

- People do business with people they like.

- Make the discussion about them, not about you.

- Ten -

One Last Piece of Advice

"I can't help but connect. I literally have to sit on my hands to stop myself."

Leigh Ann Roberts
Papa & Roberts, PLLC
Nashville, TN

Once you've mastered networking and it has become a part of your daily routine, you are ready for the NEXT (AND FINAL) STEP of our process.

If You Don't Remember Anything Else I've Said In This Book, You Must Remember This:

IT'S GOOD TO BE A NETWORKER, BUT IT'S BEST TO BE A CONNECTOR.

IF YOU AREN'T A CONNECTOR, YOU ARE MISSING BUSINESS OPPORTUNITIES!

LET ME REPEAT THIS BECAUSE IT IS IMPORTANT:

IF YOU AREN'T A CONNECTOR, YOU ARE MISSING BUSINESS OPPORTUNITIES!

While I believe that the fundamental aspect of NETWORKING is in your DNA or it isn't, I also believe that people for the most part can learn to be *CONNECTORS*.

Trust me when I say that my experience in running a high-level networking organization allows me the vantage point of seeing the results of businesspeople who have taken their game to the next level; *CONNECTOR STATUS.*

"I ask how I can help them, not how can they help me. Simple, but not something that came naturally to me."

Steve Goldstein
Advantage Business Solutions, Inc.
Nashville, TN

Some people are born to be CONNECTORS. It's in their fabric we call NETWORKING DNA. These folks are few and far between. Most of us must train ourselves to get to the next level.

IF YOU HAVE MASTERED THE SKILL OF NETWORKING, YOU CAN MASTER THE SKILLS NECESSARY TO BECOME A TOP-LEVEL CONNECTOR.

You must convince yourself that by becoming a CONNECTOR, you will take your business and its revenue to new heights.

The first thing you must do when making the leap to becoming a CONNECTOR is to throw away the idea of keeping score.

I was talking with one of my members whom I consider to be one of the top CONNECTORS in the Southeast Business Forums. I was surprised to find out that she had to teach herself this skill. One thing she told me was that for the first year or so, she experienced a very high level of frustration. Here she was making all these introductions, and nothing was coming back. She finally realized that she shouldn't be keeping score. Her frustration level decreased considerably.

Yes, part of our formal and disciplined process of networking is to keep an informal scorecard. However, when you become a CONNECTOR, you are doing something that you enjoy doing. It comes from your heart. It's like having good customer service skills.

Like my member above, if you expect a one-to-one return ratio on your introductions, you will become frustrated. Connect people because you like to connect people.

TAKE THE VIEW THAT YOUR EFFORTS WILL EVENTUALLY BE REWARDED.

It is true, and results will happen.

WHAT DOES A GOOD CONNECTOR LOOK LIKE?

"We all know people like them, people who seem to know everyone. They're always able to help, or if they can't, they know someone who can. You meet them for the first time and in 15 minutes, you're talking with them like you're childhood friends. They're successful, smart and funny, with a likable touch of self-deprecation. And they're interested in everything."
—Alina Tugend ("Are You a Connector?" SecondAct.com., December 28, 2011)

Yes, you know CONNECTORS almost as soon as you meet them:

- They are always thinking of others, including you.

- They like people and are genuinely curious (Alina Tugend).

- They have a Giver, not a Taker attitude.

- They actively connect people for a purpose.

- They are good listeners.

- They want to know more about others' business.

- They take the time to understand others' business.

- They take the time to ask their clients questions so as to identify potential opportunities to introduce their friends.

- They enjoy connecting people.

- They are willing to venture outside their comfort zones (Alina Tugend).

- They do not expect reciprocation, but they appreciate it.

"Networking I see as a means to an end. But connecting is about using a genuine love of meeting people and making friends to engage and assist one another."

Jill Leiderman
Jimmy Kimmel Live

I'll leave you with this one last thought:

CONNECTOR = The Mindset of Networking®

Good luck and good networking!

Highlights

- If you're not a connector, you are missing business opportunities.

- As a connector, you don't keep score. You appreciate the opportunity to connect people. If you do try and keep score, you will be frustrated.

- Networking is a means to an end. Connecting is a genuine love for assisting people.

- Reciprocation is not expected but is appreciated.

- Good connectors will connect people for a purpose.

- A good connector will take the time to understand your business, will remember who you need to be introduced to, and will make an effort to make those introductions.

- CONNECTOR = The Mindset of Networking®

- Appendix -

1. If I Can Do It, So Can You

In 1990 a super-regional bank purchased the small community bank that I worked for in Southern California. Up to that point in my career as a lender, my responsibilities had been to welcome the new clients brought in by the rainmakers and handle the relationships going forward. In other words, I was more of a portfolio banker than someone with any real marketing responsibilities.

One Monday morning shortly after the acquisition, the Boss stuck his head in my office and asked me, "So, what have you done for me lately?"

I said, "I don't have a pipeline, a referral base, and I've never been trained in sales."

His response was, "Well, you'd better figure it out and fast. Oh, by the way, you and the junior lender be in my office every Monday at three o'clock for our weekly marketing meeting."

So the next week, Ben and I were in the Boss's office for our weekly "marketing" meeting. He started by asking, "So, what did you do last week?"

I said, "Well, I did this, this, and this."

"That's good" was his response. "SO WHAT DID YOU BOOK?"

"Nothing."

WHAM! Out came the two-by-four across my head.

"You'd better figure out something new to do since this, this, and this isn't working," he said.

So the next week at our "marketing" meeting, the Boss asked once again, "So, what did you do last week?"

"Well, I tried something different like you said. I did that, that, and that."

Again, "That's good. SO WHAT DID YOU BOOK?"

I replied, "Nothing."

WHAM! Out came the two-by-four across my head once again.

This pattern repeated itself over the next several months with the same outcome until one Monday afternoon, I turned to Ben, the junior lender sitting beside me. The blank expression on his face told me that he had "checked out." I suppose that after so much torture one just doesn't feel the pain any longer. Ben quit several weeks later. Way to go, Boss.

I started by reaching out to my clients' accountants and attorneys. I figured they had to take my call or go to lunch with me since we shared a mutual client. Then I was introduced to a senior-level networking organization. One member in particular took me under his wing, and the first piece of advice he gave me was, "If you're starting from scratch, it will take twelve to twenty-four months before you land that first piece of significant business." At least in the banking business, he was right.

A client's attorney gave me a referral deal each time I visited with him. Every time I brought one of these deals to the Boss, he dismissed the deal (and I'm being very kind with my description of his reaction). I finally figured out that his ego and personality required him to lift his leg and "mark his territory" on each deal. In other words, he had to feel as though it was his deal. So I arranged a golf outing with the attorney, the Boss, and another lender (the Boss required this). I arranged for the Boss and the attorney to ride together, knowing that by the time we were standing on the tenth tee the attorney would have a deal for us. I was right. However, when the attorney said to the Boss, "Well, I know that my client will really like working with Stew," the Boss said, "No, I'm giving this deal to this other lender." Way to go, Boss.

I have many other examples of the "support" that my Boss gave me during this little journey. My point in telling you this is:

DON'T GIVE UP DESPITE THE HURDLES THAT THE BASTARDS THROW IN FRONT OF YOU.

I continued to listen, watch, and learn from my various networking mentors. I came to the conclusion that what I was learning really wasn't that hard. It really boiled down to common sense and perseverance. It was a process.

What I didn't realize was that the Los Angeles market at that time was experiencing a huge marketing/sales culture shift with respect to professional service provider industries, in particular the accounting and legal industries. It was like someone had flipped on a switch. All of a sudden, managing partners in legal and accounting firms were telling their young associates that the historical mandatory waiting period to become a partner no longer existed. Now to become a partner, one had to bring in business.

Immediately, senior-level networking organizations sprang up. As they evolved, it seemed that almost 70% of each chapter's membership was comprised of legal, accounting, and financial folks. The commerce going across the table was primarily between the attorneys.

The end of my story is that my networking mentors were correct. After starting from scratch, I landed one of the largest machine shops in Southern California within eighteen months. I won the "Corporate Lender of the Year" award for that year as well as the next year.

And that happened despite the best efforts of the Boss.

2. How to Construct an Effective Elevator Speech

Our process begins with our members developing a short (thirty- to forty-five-second) "elevator speech." During every meeting we ask members and guests to introduce themselves and their companies. Some are more effective than others. Some are downright lousy.

I have seen articles written by the experts who claim that the "elevator speech" is antiquated and no longer applicable. I disagree. I believe that all of us must have a fundamental introduction ready to go.

WHY DO YOU NEED IT?

You have approximately two minutes to make me remember you. That's right. You want me to *REMEMBER YOU.*

VISUAL OR PERSONAL BRAND: This is how you look to me. It is how you dress and carry and present yourself. I will determine your VISUAL BRAND in the first fifteen seconds.

VERBAL OR CORPORATE BRAND: This is how you come across to me when you speak. It is called your elevator speech. I will determine your CORPORATE BRAND from what you have to say.

WHAT ARE THE BASIC COMPONENTS?

Your Name.
Your Company's Name.
Your Defining Statement (think of this as your personal tag line).
Why Should I Schedule a Follow-up Meeting with You?

50,000 FOOT LEVEL PERSPECTIVE

MAKE IT PERSONAL: Reach me at a personal, authentic, and conversational level. You must come across without seeming to read a script or prepared commercial.

TELL ME WHAT MY PAIN IS AND HOW YOU WILL TRANSFER THAT PAIN TO YOU: No one gets business without fixing someone else's pain. So tell me what my pain is, that you understand my pain, and how you intend to fix it.

WHY WOULD I WANT TO FOLLOW UP WITH YOU?: The bottom line of your elevator speech is to get me so interested that I want to follow up with you to schedule a meeting to find out more.

WHAT DON'T YOU WANT TO DO IN YOUR ELEVATOR SPEECH?

DON'T BORE ME WITH UNNECESSARY DETAILS.

I DON'T CARE about how many employees you have or where your office is or how many years your company has been in business. Leave those details to your follow-up meeting.

LET'S BEGIN TO CONSTRUCT YOUR ELEVATOR SPEECH.

FIRST, YOUR NAME.
Easy, right? I hope so.

Example One:
Hi, my name is Joel Widmer.

Example Two:
Hi, my name is Terry Humphrey.

Example Three:
My name is Dan Aronoff.

SECOND, YOUR COMPANY'S NAME.

Harder than the first one but still relatively easy. How can you butcher the name of your company?

Example One:
I run a company named Fluxe Digital Marketing.

Example Two:
The name of my company is Terry Humphrey, LLC.

Example Three:
My company's name is Frannet.

THIRD, YOUR DEFINING STATEMENT.

Okay, here's where it begins to get harder.

Example One:
I'm a geek. But what makes me different from the thousands of other geeks out there is that I know how to effectively put technology and business together.

Example Two:
I eliminate the trash floating around in your head.

Example Three:
I'm a franchise matchmaker.

FOURTH, GIVE ME A REASON TO FOLLOW UP WITH YOU.

This is the hardest part to come up with.

Example One:
What I do is take a business owner's computer and turn it into the most productive salesperson on his or her staff.

Example Two:
What I do is help people clean out their head trash so they can concentrate on doing what is most important and that is achieving the goals they have set for themselves and their business. I provide solutions through executive and business coaching.

Example Three:
There's more to franchise businesses than French fries. I help people who want to take off their corporate shackles and run their own business. I do this by matching them with the best opportunity that fits their needs.

Okay, the defining statements in these examples are very good ones. Each one makes you remember who that person is. In Example Three, Dan's the "Franchise Matchmaker." Will you remember Terry (Example Two) as the person who eliminates someone's head trash? You bet you will!

Now think about Joel's last statement above (Example One). He hasn't told you what he does, has he? No, what he's done is tell you that he takes a computer and turns it into a salesperson and not just a salesperson but also the highest-producing salesperson in the company. Don't you want to have a second meeting with him to find out how he does that? Don't you think your clients might be interested in something like this? Don't you think that if you introduce Joel to your client you'll look like a hero to the client?

LAST COMMENT ON THIS: WHERE IN ANY OF THESE ELEVATOR SPEECHES DID THEY TELL YOU WHERE THEIR OFFICE IS, HOW MANY EMPLOYEES THEY HAVE, OR THEIR YEARS IN BUSINESS?

NOWHERE!

WHY? BECAUSE YOU DON'T CARE, AND IT ADDS NOTHING TO WHY YOU WOULD WANT TO FOLLOW UP WITH THEM.

EVERY ELEVATOR SPEECH HAS TO BE CRAFTED DIFFERENTLY.

Your business is not like other people's business. But for sake of the elevator speech, it is. What do I mean by this?

You must determine the best way to connect using the elevator speech.

For some business verticals, a different approach will be used compared to others. For example, I think everyone understands what a banker, an attorney, a wealth manager, an insurance agent, and an accountant do. Therefore, constructing an elevator speech built around WHAT THEY DO is a big waste of time. What they need to say is HOW THEY DIFFERENTIATE themselves from the other bankers, lawyers, wealth managers, insurance agents and accountants.

Now take the person who delivers products and services in the employee benefits and executive compensation vertical. Not many people really understand what this is. If you did (with all due respect to my friends in this line of work), you'll think that it's really boring. So if they build an elevator speech around what they do, I'll zone out. They have to take a different approach than the banker et al.

In either case (or in between), constructing the right defining statement will be critical.

One of our members tells his story in terms of how businesses do four things: make money, save money, become more efficient, and try to stay out of the courtroom. He says that he takes care of three of the four by taking on those issues so as to free up the business owner to go out and concentrate on making money.

What has he done in his elevator speech? He's told me what my pain points are and that he will transfer them from my shoulders onto his. He then tells me the benefit of his doing this – "I will make more money by freeing up time."

Another member recognizes her audience is older and is struggling with social media and how to wrap their arms around it as an overall marketing tool. So she begins by telling the audience exactly what they are thinking and sympathizing with them. Then she tells the audience how she will fix their pain.

What has she done up front? She got the audience's attention by bringing the problem down to them on a personal level. Essentially by saying, "I feel your pain."

CONSISTENCY

Over time, one of the key factors to getting the desired results is CONSISTENCY. Once you're comfortable with the fundamental structure of your elevator speech make sure you deliver the message on a consistent basis.

"I have found that the person who gives me one or two MAIN and consistent points (at each meeting) is very helpful. But when a person tries to cover ALL things, it is difficult for me to follow, let alone remember. Over time, I feel comfortable referring to the person who has a short message because I feel confident that I can tell my client what they do."

Ivie Burns II
Morgan Stanley
Franklin, TN

WRITE, REWRITE, AND THEN REWRITE SOME MORE.

If you come up with your elevator speech after one attempt at writing, then the odds of its being successful are pretty small.

You will likely find yourself rewriting the speech many, many times before you are satisfied. That's okay and should be expected.

PRACTICE, PRACTICE AND THEN PRACTICE SOME MORE.

Practice your elevator speech until it becomes second nature to you. At that point, you will feel comfortable with it, it won't sound like a commercial, and it won't sound like you're straining to get the message out.

Try doing these little tricks:

- Write the speech multiple times.

- Stand in front of a mirror and practice.

- Call yourself up and give the speech to your voice mail. Then retrieve the voice mail and listen to yourself.

- Practice in front of a loved one.

- Then practice in front of someone who doesn't love you. Pick the person who you think has mastered her elevator speech and you think will be honest and objective with her feedback.

ADAPT TO YOUR SURROUNDINGS.

Having a core elevator speech is fundamental to being able to adapt to the crowd you are addressing. You need to be able to contract or expand your elevator pitch. You need to be able to massage the pitch depending on the type of crowd (e.g., higher level of sophistication or less; industry versus general audience). You may want to consider the message that you want to leave your audience with and then adapt the speech to meet that goal.

The pitch you give when standing up in a networking group will likely be different than your introduction in a room full of your competition at an industry association meeting. Your elevator speech at a cocktail party one-on-one will likely be less than thirty seconds. So be prepared with the short version of your speech.

The core elevator speech gives you the benchmark from which to make those adjustments. Without it, you are not sending a consistent and straightforward message.

LISTEN AND EVALUATE OTHER ELEVATOR SPEECHES.

What is a better way to learn than by listening to and evaluating other elevator speeches?

Here's a good litmus test: Did the defining statement cause me to ask, "How do you do that?" or say, "Tell me more"?

In your mind, critique each of the speeches you hear. Ask yourself if the speech met the basic components that were outlined earlier. Did the speaker add a bunch of stuff that was worthless information to you? Did that speaker pique your interest enough to want to schedule a follow-up meeting? If the answer to that last question was "No," then he didn't do a very good job.

After a while you will be able to quickly pick up on the good elevator speeches and, I hope, be able to incorporate some of those points in your speech.

ONE LAST THING.

Here's a comment from Seth Godin that one of my members sent me and I will leave you with this:

"NO ONE EVER BOUGHT ANYTHING ON AN ELEVATOR."

"If your elevator pitch is a hyper-compressed two-minute overview of your hopes, dreams and the thing you've been building for the last three years, you're doing everyone a disservice.

"The best elevator pitch doesn't pitch your project. It pitches the meeting about your project. The best elevator pitch is true, stunning, brief and it leaves the listener eager (no, desperate) to hear the rest of it. It's not a practiced, polished turd of prose that pleases everyone on the board and your marketing team, it's a little fractal of the entire story, something real."

3. E-mail Introduction

I like to make introductions via e-mail. I try to standardize the structure of the e-mail to maintain some consistency. Here's a sample of an e-mail introduction that I commonly use.

E-MAIL INTRODUCTION:

Good afternoon, Joel and Susan:

I'd like to take this opportunity to introduce you to one another.

Joel, as I mentioned to you, Susan and her company built and now run our website. I know that you've been on it and were impressed with its functionality. Susan, Joel runs a digital strategy marketing company. I thought that the two of you may have some good synergy.

>Joel Widmer
>Fluxe Digital Marketing
>615.222.3333
>joel@hisbusinessname.com

>Susan Web
>Web Marketing
>615.222.3334
>susan@herbusinessname.com

>Good luck and good networking.

>Stew

Yes, it's long. But you've made the commitment to introduce two people that you feel strongly should get together. SO TAKE THE TIME AND DO IT RIGHT.

- I took the time to mention WHY I thought it was important that they should meet. I hope this takes care of the meaningless introductions (i.e., introductions just for the sake of introducing).

- I provided them with each other's contact information. In fact, I gave them TWO different ways to contact each other. Don't leave them high and dry. It's not professional, and you have likely wasted any goodwill you've built with the mere act of introducing them.

- I left them with a slogan.

4. Response to an E-mail Introduction

Okay, now that you've received the actual introduction, what's your response going to be? Again, I use a standardized response. It doesn't have to be long.

E-MAIL RESPONSE:

Good afternoon, Susan. First of all, a BIG thank you to Stew for making this introduction. It is greatly appreciated.

Susan, I'd like to get together over a cup of coffee to learn more about your business. Please let me know a couple of dates and times that fit into your schedule.

Thanks, I look forward to hearing from you shortly.

      Joel Widmer

5. The "One-Sheet" and How to Construct It

In 1991 when I joined the networking group in Los Angeles, social media did not exist in the way it does today. I can't even remember if websites existed then. If they did, a company with one was certainly on the cutting edge. Today, websites are like business cards. You are expected to have one because if you don't, your credibility suffers.

Back then, each of us created what we called the "One-Sheet." It was a one-page piece of paper that we would hand out at formal networking meetings, Troika meetings, and other appropriate occasions.

The effective "One-Sheet" would be professionally produced (using higher grade paper, perhaps professionally designed, perhaps printed commercially, etc.). It would contain my picture (in business attire) and would address KEY AND IMPORTANT information that I wanted the reader to remember about me.

Today, most marketing professionals will tell you that you must drive your audience to your company's website. It is there that you can "tell your story." I don't disagree. However, I believe the "One-Sheet" is still a powerful tool if it is constructed properly and used at appropriate times. One advantage today compared to more than twenty years ago is the digital storage of information.

Here is an example of my "One-Sheet."

STEWART C. ROSS

EXECUTIVE DIRECTOR
SOUTHEAST BUSINESS FORUMS, LLC

Southeast Business Forums is a senior-level, professional service provider networking organization. We are strictly "Business-to-Business."

Our culture is rooted in "The Mindset of Networking®," a formal and disciplined approach to networking. We believe strongly in developing deep and long lasting relationships that, over time, will result in meaningful introductions, referrals and commerce. Our culture is built on the philosophy of being a giver and not a taker.

If you are tired of networking organizations that are "Business-to-Consumer," rely on quick hit methods and promote a culture of being a taker, you will want to consider the Southeast Business Forums.

Your next step is to visit one of our monthly chapter meetings and experience a different approach to networking . . . one that produces results.

As your sponsoring member, I will ensure that you receive a formal invitation to the meeting of your choice. You may contact me at the following:

Stewart C. Ross
615.887.0892
stew.ross@southeastbusinessforums.com

Please visit us at www.southeastbusinessforums.com and take a moment to view our videos. You will see that the Southeast Business Forums is a networking organization that over delivers for its members.

I also invite you to visit our blog site at blog@themindsetofnetworking.com. Please subscribe and receive the regular content that our members contribute.

Mr. Ross is a retired commercial banker. He started the Business Forums in January 2007. In his spare time, he writes and publishes books. His most recent book, "*The Mindset of Networking®*," will be published in 2013. He is also working on a series of niche travel guides. The first in the series, "*Where Did They Put The Guillotine?*," will be published in early 2014. Mr. Ross and his wife enjoy traveling, collecting fine art and enjoy time with their grandchildren.

Your FIRST STEP is to create the "One-Sheet." The process is almost similar to creating your personal elevator speech.

- Your picture in high resolution

- Your contact information

- Name

- Address

- Phone/Cell Number

- E-Mail Address

- Website Address

- Briefly encapsulate what you do

- Tell me the problems that you fix for your clients

- If you can, impress me with the names of some clients

- Above all, PUT SOMETHING IN IT THAT I WILL REMEMBER YOU BY. Remember the *Defining Statement* mentioned earlier? That's a good place to start.

Now, are you going to create this on your own, use inferior paper stock, print it on your home printer, and hope it works? I'd tell you *NO, ABSOLUTELY NOT!*

Why? Because my personal philosophy is that if something is not professional in its appearance, effect, and overall standing, you've wasted your time. Yes, I know that we are all dealing with budgets, but think about the impression that someone leaves you with when he presents you with a business card that is not professional. Remember our discussions about personal branding?

STORY

I met a very knowledgeable management consultant who specialized in helping people get started with their first business. He handed me his card. The next time we got together, I had to be honest with him. I asked him, "Why would I hire you to help me start my business when your business card looks like it came right off your home printer, a very weak paper bond, less than professional design, AND your address is an apartment building." The next time we met, his new business cards were professionally done.

ADVICE Have your "One-Sheet" professionally designed and printed commercially. This is the same advice I'd give anyone concerning logo, business cards, marketing collateral material, or ANYTHING you would want to present on a professional basis.

Your NEXT STEP is to determine when to use the "One-Sheet." We determined that the best time to distribute it would be at the Troika meetings (or any meetings when several people get together to know one another a little better).

You must accept that almost all the people who receive your "One-Sheet" will likely throw it away. So you ask, "Why give it to them?" The answer is two-fold. First, you must put something in it that will make them remember you by. BEFORE YOU LEAVE THE MEETING, MAKE SURE YOU POINT OUT WHAT YOU WANT THEM TO REMEMBER YOU BY.

Second, you will ask them before you leave the meeting whether they would like to receive a digital version of your "One-Sheet." More and more people are creating files for such stuff. If your guest doesn't do this, wouldn't this be an opportune time for you to suggest it and say, "Oh, by the way, why don't you use my 'One-Sheet' as your first file?"